MARKS OF THE CROSS

EMBRACING THE CHARACTER OF CHRIST

ROBERT J. GLADSTONE

HEAVEN RULES

CONTENTS

Introduction	1
1. Wisdom	11
2. Rest	23
3. Meekness	33
4. Humility	52
5. Forgiveness	84
6. The Marks of Maturity	102
Also by Robert J. Gladstone	115

© 2020 by Robert J. Gladstone

Marks of the Cross

Embracing the Character of Christ

Heaven Rules Publications

Charlotte, NC

thekingspeople.org

Cover Design by Kathleen Dunnam and Evan Gladstone

Interior Design by SteveBremner.com

All Rights reserved under International Copyright Law. No part of this book may be reproduced or transmitted in any form or by any means, electronic or mechanical—including photocopying, recording, or by any information storage and retrieval system—without permission in writing from the publisher.

Unless otherwise noted, all Scripture quotations are taken from the New American Standard Bible. Copyright © 1960, 1962, 1963, 1968, 1971, 1973, 1975, 1977, 1995 by the Lockman Foundation. Used by Permission.

Scripture quotations marked LEB are from the Lexham English Bible. Copyright 2012 Logos Bible Software. Lexham is a registered trademark of Logos Bible Software.

Scripture quotations marked NIV®, or NIV84, are taken from the Holy Bible, New International Version. Copyright © 1973, 1978, 1984, 2011 by Biblica, Inc.® Used by permission. All rights reserved worldwide.

Scripture quotations marked CSB are taken from the Christian Standard Bible. Copyright © 2017 by Holman Bible Publishers. Used by permission. Christian Standard Bible®, and CSB® are federally registered trademarks of Holman Bible Publishers, all rights reserved.

Scripture quotations marked ESV are taken from the Holy Bible, English Standard Version®. ESV® Text Edition: 2016. Copyright © 2001 by Crossway, a publishing ministry of Good News Publishers. The ESV® text has been reproduced in cooperation with and by permission of Good News Publishers. Unauthorized reproduction of this publication is prohibited. All rights reserved.

Scripture quotations marked NKJV are taken from THE HOLY BIBLE, New King James Version®, copyright © 1982 by Thomas Nelson. Used by permission. All rights reserved.

Scripture quotations marked NCV are taken from the New Century Version®. Copyright © 2005 by Thomas Nelson. Used by permission. All rights reserved.

Print ISBN: 978-1-7349821-0-7

Ebook ISBN: 978-1-7349821-1-4

Printed in the United States of America

For Finley

INTRODUCTION
MARKED BY LOVE

"We boast in the hope of the glory of God!"

So says Paul, virtually singing a refrain from the symphony of wonders found in the gospel (Rom 5:2, LEB). He's overcome with confidence and joy as he considers the overwhelming grace of the good news. He has discovered that the gospel gives him unlimited spiritual benefits that make it impossible to complain or lose heart. He knows he doesn't deserve the glorious hope he now possesses. Yet by the grace of Jesus Christ he has received it. Now the meaning of life is answered. The heart's deepest desires are fulfilled, will always be fulfilled, and will forever be increasingly fulfilled. Paul swims in an ocean of spiritual delight, a sea so immense and crystal clear that he cannot imagine life on the land of the old creation again. His gratitude is immeasurable and his rapture irrepressible. For Paul, and all who would believe, nothing from the outside can alter this glorious hope. He has profound reason to boast.

Yet it gets even better. Not only does Paul boast in the hope of God's glory, but in the very next verse, he also boasts in his "tribulations" (Rom 5:3).

It's easy to understand why Paul would boast about hope. But how could he boast about, even find joy in, tribulations? How did he see the silver lining around the clouds of trouble and hardship, persecution and famine, nakedness and danger that his life as a gospel missionary brought him (Rom 8:35)? It's not like he occasionally felt a little pressure or hit a few bumps in the road. Paul's suffering was extreme (2 Cor 11:13-29).

Synagogue officials had struck his back with a whip 39 times on *five* occasions (that's 195 strokes). An angry mob pounded his body with a hailstorm of large rocks, apparently killing him, after which God raised him back up (see Acts 14:19-20). One night he spent draped over a piece of wood in the middle of the ocean. He constantly traveled in difficult conditions, in continual danger, under persistent pressure—at times running for his life. He was forced to endure betrayal and slander by many of his own Jewish people, former Christian friends, and strangers in strange lands. Did Paul really relish these tribulations? Was he psychotic?

No, actually, Paul was sober-minded and clear-sighted. Not only did he see the eternal glory awaiting him on the other side of such trouble, but he saw its potential effect on his character *now*. So valuable was that effect that it made life worth the trouble. For Paul, the whole point of living was not to have comfort and ease on a temporary earth; it was to become more like Jesus. He wrote with bottom-line insight:

"Those whom He foreknew, He also predestined to become conformed to the image of His Son" (Rom 8:29).

Christ-like character was Paul's destiny, the meaning of life itself. So if tribulations got deep into his soul, carving more and more of Christ's image into it, and if Paul allowed such carving to occur every time life struck a blow to his body or heart, then we can see why he boasted in his tribulations. Paul valued character and eternity over this world and temporary pleasure. Suffering did not mar his vision of the Kingdom; it helped him see it.

But let's be clear. Paul never claimed that God sent terrible things into his life to make him more like Jesus. Nor am I claiming that. Paul's worst troubles came through satanic forces or rebellious people.[1] However, Paul knew that God could take attacks from the enemy and reroute them into His purpose. As Joseph said, "As for you, you meant evil against me, but God meant it for good…" (Gen 50:20). And Paul himself said, "We know that all things work together for the good of those who love God, who are called according to his purpose" (Rom 8:28, CSB). Paul did not blame God for sending evil and suffering into his life. But he did rejoice that God could take those assaults and force their effects into the divine goal of Christ-like character.

To become like Jesus was Paul's purpose and greatest joy. And by God's amazing grace, unfathomable wisdom, and glorious gospel, Paul knew even his troubles could help make him like Jesus. That is how he boasted about those troubles, despite their pain. Hence, Paul sang for joy both in response to his hope of glory *and* the potential benefits of adversity. Gospel life redeems everything. No matter pit, prison, pain, prosperity, or pleasure, the gospel thwarted every kind of regret and gave Paul reason to rejoice in the fulfillment of God's purpose: to be conformed to the image of His Son.

Now we can read these precious words and, by the Spirit of life that breathed them into Scripture, possess the same hope when life brings us wounds—even wounds that leave permanent marks.

Scars are a part of life. Betrayals, trials, and troubles in this fallen world will wound our souls. For Jesus' followers in particular, He taught us that we would have tribulation in the world and that affliction or persecution would come "because of the word" (John 16:33; Mark 4:17). The Kingdom way of life will often be repaid with resistance or sinful reactions that hurt, offend, or even oppress us. We cannot live and love well in this world without injury. But take heart: if we really do follow Jesus, and if we allow His Spirit to work in our lives through the pain, those wounds heal into scars.

And scars become character.

As a result, healed wounds can become signposts to something greater. But we must determine whether or not they do. We must steward the pain, so to speak, allowing resistance to become a hammer and God's Word a chisel that mold us into the image of His Son. Then the wounds turn into scars, and scars constitute our character. I call them the marks of the cross.

A Visitor from China

Many years ago, Brother Yun, the Chinese house church leader imprisoned and tortured for his faith, visited our church in North Carolina. Before the service he met privately with our leadership team. It was a meeting I will not forget.[2]

Through his translator, Yun told how policemen and prison guards beat his legs below the knees so severely that they left them broken, black, and crippled. Agony replaced his ability to walk. Fellow prisoners had to carry him between his cell, the torture room, and the bathroom. But one morning the Lord gave him a vision about his release, telling him the hour of his salvation had come. Iron doors opened miraculously, guards were blinded, and Yun freely walked through the prison to the street where a taxi drove up and took him to his friends' apartment.

Only after his arrival did it dawn on him that he was healed. He had been using his legs since he walked out of his cell. As he shared this part of the story, Yun lifted his trousers above the ankles. Like drawing a veil that concealed sacred script, he showed us the scars from his torture.

The sight was jarring. Vandalized flesh bespoke the cruelty of Yun's torturers and his own unthinkable pain. But there was a deeper message. The distortions on his legs were no longer wounds; they were scars. The wounds had mended into signs of suffering *that had healed into a new form.* Now they were marks of character—Christ's character branded through the skin into his soul.

But by looking beneath the surface of Yun's physical scars, I do not mean to trivialize the external pain of his torture. I honor him for enduring things of which we believers in the West know precious little. Yun's scars are the marks of Jesus branded in his body (Gal 6:17). They are his glory, testifying to his extreme sacrifice and placing him among the great heroes of the faith.

Still, the bodily torture does not mean Yun's scars lack deeper meaning. Scripture teaches that physical suffering must correspond to internal character. "If I surrender my body to be burned, but do have not love, it profits me nothing" (1 Cor 13:3).

Yun was privileged to have both. His scars were more than physical marks; they were internal signs marking the moments of injustice when he chose the way of the cross. Every time he risked his neck for the gospel, every time he suffered for the Name, every time he forgave his torturers, every time he served his fellow prisoners—*every* act of self-denial left a scar on his heart from which a bud of Jesus' character, the fruit of the Holy Spirit, emerged.

Not all believers have the marks of the cross on their bodies. But all true disciples must have the marks of the cross on their souls. They mark the moments when we allowed some pain to become a path into the mystery of the cross. They mark every time we suffered the loss of one of our rights in order to walk the way of the Messiah. That is what forges His character into our souls, and that is the way of grace. Jesus paid the price to give us new life without cost. But now He calls us to make the necessary sacrifices to work that gift of new life into our daily thoughts, relationships, behavior, and witness (Acts 14:22; 2 Pet 1:3-11).

Christ's character is costly. It requires sacrifice and loss.

It leaves scars.

The Master's Workshop

Resistance, after all, is the workshop in which the Master Craftsman does His finest work. Those who recognize this and dare to convert their wounds into scars emerge as gold purified by fire.

Disciples with scars are real. Their sonship was granted freely but not developed cheaply. They are branded by fire—purchased with precious blood but matured in a cauldron. The power of their character cannot be faked. They have faced betrayal and frustration, disappointment and struggle. Like metal softened by blue-hot flames, they were prepared for the strikes of hammer and chisel to shape them into Messiah's image.

> All discipline for the moment seems not to be joyful, but sorrowful; yet to those who have been trained by it, afterwards it yields the peaceful fruit of righteousness (Heb 12:11).

Even in His resurrected body, Jesus Christ still has scars. Eternity refuses to remove the marks of His death, choosing rather to glorify them. Jesus' scars remain, not only as memorials to the price of eternal salvation, but also as signs of His eternal character. Why should His glorified body hide

His scars? Resurrection does not erase them; resurrection confirms them. Jesus' scars forever reveal the essence of His character: sacrificial, covenantal love.

That is why Paul determined to know nothing except Jesus Christ as crucified (1 Cor 2:2; Gal 3:1)—not because Jesus was still in the grave, but because *He still bears scars*. Jesus always was, always is, and always will be the one who loved enough to pay the ultimate price. Crucifixion is more than the way Jesus died in history; it is His essential character, and He has the scars to prove it. In that sense, He is forever the Crucified One. The stigma of crucifixion became the glory of love. "For love is strong as death, jealousy is fierce as the grave" (Song 8:6, ESV).

It is the same for those who follow Him. Whether or not we have the privilege to bear physical scars, we must bear the scars of the Messiah's character on our souls. We must pay the price to cultivate His nature in our lives.

> If anyone would come after me, let him deny himself and take up his cross and follow me. For whoever would save his life will lose it, but whoever loses his life for my sake will find it. For what will it profit a man if he gains the whole world and forfeits his soul? Or what shall a man give in return for his soul? For the Son of Man is going to come with his angels in the glory of his Father, and then he will repay each person according to what he has done. Truly, I say to you, there are some standing here who will not taste death until they see the Son of Man coming in his kingdom (Matt 16:24-28, ESV).

The Scars

So what are these scars, these marks on those who take up their crosses and follow Jesus? They are the character traits of Jesus that sprout from the soil of loss. Jesus is *the* Crucified One—the one whose lifestyle we must cultivate into our own. The love that marked His life must now mark our lives.

> I have been crucified with Christ. It is no longer I who live, but Christ who lives in me. And the life I now live in the flesh I live by faith in the Son of God, *who loved me and gave himself for me* (Gal 2:20, ESV, emphasis added).

> For those whom he foreknew he also predestined to be conformed to the image of his Son, in order that he might be the firstborn among many brothers (Rom 8:29, ESV).

We have been raised to new life, and that life is Christ himself. We bear His image. That means the marks of His selfless character—marks He still bears in glory—must also mark our character. When we cultivate life in the Spirit, we will bear the marks of His cross.

Five "marks" stand out to me and make up the contents of this book. They are five virtues that in my experience require sacrifice to develop in the Spirit while unlocking doors to Jesus' many other character traits. When we allow them to mark our lives, they bring with them the practical power of Jesus' resurrection. On my journey of faith so far, I have discovered these to be five crucial marks of the cross:

- *Wisdom* — The way of life that flows from God's

unique knowledge and value system, exposing the conventional "wisdom" of this world as folly.

- *Rest* — Total peace in Christ that conquers anxiety and empowers us to perform God's works with faith.

- *Meekness* — A gentle character whose only agenda consists of God's will, allowing us to inherit later what the world pursues with aggression now.

- *Humility* — The spirit of love and generous servanthood that demolishes the need for self-promotion and waits for God to exalt us.

- *Forgiveness* — The heart of the cross' gracious, pardoning justice that heals relationships and liberates us from anger, bitterness, and resentment.

What follows are some practical thoughts on each of these marks. I hope they will help you cultivate the same character traits in your own life. I believe they represent aspects of the crucified and risen Jesus Christ that, when embodied by His people, will change the world.

---

1. See Acts 9:23-24; 13:45, 50; 14:2-6, 19; 17:5-9, 13; 18:12; 19:23-41; 21:27-36; 22:22; 23:1-2, 12-14; 2 Cor 12:7; 1 Thess 2:14-16.
2. For more on the story that follows, see Brother Yun and Paul Hattaway, *The Heavenly Man: The Remarkable True Story of Chinese Christian Brother Yun* (Oxford: Monarch Books, 2002) 212-229.

1

WISDOM

The cross of Christ represents a divine, selfless lifestyle at complete odds with the spirit of our age. Such a lifestyle is what the Bible calls "wisdom." Wisdom is the practical knowledge of God's utterly unique value system translated into a powerful, blessed way of life. But we must remember that God's wisdom is not like the world's wisdom. What the world calls wise, successful, and powerful, God calls foolish, fruitless, and feeble. Conversely, what God calls wise and powerful, the world calls foolish and weak.

In God's mind, the cross of Christ is wisdom—a wisdom that confounds the wise of this age. Therefore, to live according to God's cross-shaped wisdom requires the sacrifice of our old, natural ways and will often create friction with the world around us. Such sacrifices will leave scars. Which is why I consider wisdom a mark of the cross.

> For the word of the cross is foolishness to those who are perishing, but to us who are being saved it is the power of God. For it is written, "I will destroy the wisdom of the wise, and the cleverness of the clever I will set aside" (1 Cor 1:18-19).

The crucifixion of Jesus Christ displayed the awesome wisdom of God to the whole world. In response, however, the world saw it as anything *but* wisdom. Rulers of this age saw the cross as sheer folly, as absolute madness: a man claiming to be God's Son, the King of Israel, dying like a villain and fool—unclothed, undignified, unsung.

Is that how the God of all love, knowledge, and power operates? Is that the way He reveals Himself and rescues His people? Is that how He presents the King to whom we should pledge our allegiance?

But Jesus tells us, "Wisdom is vindicated by her deeds" (Matt 11:19).

What looked like shame and insanity on that fateful day became, in fact, the vehicle of eternal salvation when God raised Jesus from the dead and enthroned Him over all creation. Through defeat came victory, through weakness came strength, through humiliation came glory, through death came life. Yes, wisdom was indeed vindicated by her deeds.

As a result, a crucial question stares humanity in the face. Will we embrace this wisdom? Will we humble ourselves, admitting how foolish, weak, and utterly useless our philosophies of life and religion have been? Will we follow the narrow path of the strange, divine wisdom embodied by the cross, rejected by the world but accepted by God?

Our failure to answer this question well has become the blight of frail Christianity. If we are not willing to embrace the folly of the cross, neither can we encounter its wisdom. If we will not embrace its weakness, we cannot tap into its power (1 Cor 1:20-25).

How often we have tried to benefit from the cross' wisdom and power without welcoming its folly and weakness! Western Christianity has sanitized the cross to make it palatable. We've become experts at taking its shocking reality and polishing it into a religious symbol on a steeple, a piece of fine art around our necks, or a cool graphic on our church video screens, rather than the radical, God-centered, selfless, meek, and antithetical lifestyle that it is. We should beware this temptation.

The cross is severe, it is brutal, and it is ugly. It is God's rebuke to human wisdom. In the ancient Roman Empire, it was a savage, scandalous way to die. But it became God's chosen instrument for his Son's atoning death. As such, it reveals God's wisdom while destroying ours.

> *When we in our foolishness thought we were wise*
> *He played the fool and He opened our eyes*
> *When we in our weakness believed we were strong*
> *He became helpless to show we were wrong.*[1]

What, then, does God's wisdom look like in everyday life?

The Wisdom of the Cross Values Eternity

> Fixing our eyes on Jesus, the author and perfecter of faith, who for the joy set before Him endured the cross, despising the shame, and has sat down at the right hand of the throne of God (Heb 12:2).

Roman crucifixion was dreadful. For Jesus it was six hours of torture and agony. Yet the cross was God's plan of salvation—the only way for Jesus to gain the breathtaking, eternal joy awaiting Him. And that blissful hope is what enabled Jesus to brave His brutal death.

Through the pain of His passion, Jesus' heart beat for the joy of being clothed with an immortal, resurrection body. His mind imagined the satisfaction of soaring through the heavens, ascending far above defeated enemies, and taking His throne at the Father's right hand. What pleasure He anticipated when angels would sing for joy during His cosmic enthronement. Even as He suffered, His inner eyes saw the Day when He would return to earth and judge the nations, make right every wrong, eliminate all evil, and renew creation. Sheer delight filled His soul as He envisioned His glorious bride, the church, without spot or wrinkle or any such thing.

Yes, Jesus' death would lead to great joy for Him. It was the "joy set before Him" that provided the power to endure the shame and brutality of crucifixion. The same pattern applies to us. Vision of our glorious future empowers us to yield to God's will today.

> For I consider that the sufferings of this present time are not worthy to be compared with the glory that is to be revealed to us… For in hope we have been saved, but hope that is seen is not hope; for who hopes for what he already sees? But if we hope for what we do not see, with perseverance we wait eagerly for it (Rom 8:18, 24).

We cannot carry our cross as a lifestyle unless the joys of eternity are real to our hearts (Matt 16:24-28). Wisdom sees eternity and lives by the light of its hope. Wisdom conducts itself in this world as if resurrection is real, judgment is real, eternity is real, and reward is real. This is what the Bible calls the "living hope" to which we were born again through Jesus Christ's resurrection (1 Pet 1:3). *Wisdom lives in the light of eternity.* Gospel hope is no fantasy or escape from reality. It *is* reality. It is spiritual common sense, just as denial of such a hope is the worst kind of foolishness. One day we will rise. Then in one moment—in a flash faster than a bolt of lightning—everything in this life will be vaporized, and only what we invested into Christ's Kingdom will remain.

Wisdom, then, allows the joy of our eternal *future* to infuse and inspire the way we live *now*. That is why the cross embodies wisdom. It recognizes—indeed, it declares—that this age is passing away and that the coming age is wonderfully eternal and eternally wonderful. *That* perspective is God's wisdom by which we can and must live now.

So we no longer make major decisions or respond to problems as if this world were our home. Rather, cross-centered wisdom values the urgencies of eternity over the urgencies of this world. It *rejoices* in the prospects of eternal reward and therefore has the energy to live contrary to the selfish demands of this world's justice and values. For the joy set before it, this wisdom lives meekly amid mayhem, forgives relentlessly amid injustice, and serves selflessly amid conceit.

> Therefore, my beloved brethren, be steadfast, immovable, always abounding in the work of the Lord, knowing that *your toil is not in vain* in the Lord (1 Cor 15:58, emphasis added).

The Wisdom of the Cross Exchanges Human Weakness for the Power of the Spirit

> I determined to know nothing among you except Jesus Christ, and Him crucified. I was with you in weakness and in fear and in much trembling, and my message and my preaching were not in persuasive words of wisdom, but in demonstration of the Spirit and of power (1 Cor 2:2-4).

The apostle Paul was a powerful man. Not only did he leave behind a legacy of churches scattered throughout the Mediterranean world, but he helped change history through the influence of those churches, his preaching, and of course his letters that have been canonized as Scripture. Much of his thought remains impressed into the wax of many cultures today. It has affected worldviews, governments, philosophies, art, and literature. But most importantly, for generations his writings have brought indescribable freedom to those who have believed the gospel he preached.

His was a trail blazed for the ages. Fruit from his Kingdom work will last forever to God's glory.

Marks of the Cross

What was the secret to his success? How did the life of this one man, a physically unimpressive former Pharisee, have such a lasting impact on his world? The secret to Paul's success was the raw power of the Holy Spirit. There is no other way for any of us to have authentic, eternal impact on the people around us. It is only by the anointing of the Holy Spirit.

We must, therefore, discover how Paul manifested the Spirit so powerfully and consistently in his life: he did it by living according to God's wisdom exemplified in the "word of the cross" (1 Cor 1:18).

The cross declares that God's wisdom is a paradox to the natural human mind. It is an odd blend of weakness and power. It is God's rebuke to the wisdom of this world—a wisdom rooted in human pride that boasts its strength before God. For God's wisdom does not seek a successful life through ambition at the expense of others. Nor does it seek to build a ministry based on popularity, good looks, skilled speech, or human ingenuity. Rather, it accentuates human *weakness* as the open door to the Holy Spirit's presence and power.

God's wisdom, therefore, is life in the Spirit. If we want to live by God's wisdom, we must accept that the Holy Spirit resists all forms of pride. The Spirit is like an innocent dove who naturally shies away from the shoulders of vanity and self-reliance. Instead, the Spirit loves humility and meekness. He is attracted to the attributes embodied in the cross carried by God's Son.

This is the wisdom of the cross. It values the Spirit's presence and power so highly, it will do nothing to drive Him away while doing everything to attract Him. Jesus' cross embodied this unique wisdom. To human eyes, His death looked like foolishness, weakness, shame, and defeat. But God looked upon such radical humility and anointed it, raising Jesus from the dead in triumph, glory, power, and wisdom.

Paul recognized this pattern of death-to-resurrection as God's distinctive wisdom. So he embraced it as the model for his entire life and ministry. God calls us to do the same.

Jesus is our example of this wisdom. He lived His life as the symmetrical opposite to human pride. He willingly took the role of a servant, defying the expectations of both Jews and Gentiles in the way He expressed His majesty. His Father's plan demanded it. Sin, death, and the devil could never be conquered by religious piety, human schemes, or military might. No, Jesus conquered the powers of darkness by dying on a cross, looking frail and foolish.

> The foolishness of God is wiser than men and the weakness of God is stronger than men (1 Cor 1:25).

As a follower of Jesus, Paul well expressed this paradox. In order to manifest the *power* of God's Spirit, he went out of his way to boast about his *weaknesses*.

> Most gladly, therefore, I will rather boast about my weaknesses, so that the power of Christ may dwell in me. Therefore I am well content with weaknesses, with insults, with distresses, with persecutions, with difficulties, for Christ's sake; for when I am weak, then I am strong (2 Cor 12:9-10).

Paul's personal weaknesses created the platform on which God displayed the miraculous wonders of the Messiah. But why? What is it about human weakness that allows God's power to work so freely?

Because if God can empower weak, human vessels like us, then clearly, *He alone is God.* Put another way, when we frail ones live in divine virtue and perform divine works, the attention goes to God, not us. "But we have this treasure in jars of clay to show that this all-surpassing power is from God and not from us" (2 Cor 4:7, NIV). When humans come to such a place—against their natural pride, against the whole spirit of a world system declaring its independence from God—that they utterly need God for everything, then God can show the world *through them* that He is God.

God makes weak people powerful and powerful people weak.

This is exactly why, throughout his letters, Paul lists his weaknesses. He does not boast in his great exploits as an apostle in order to impress people. (Or at least, when he does, he calls it "foolishness" and does it only because he was "forced" to do so by immature church members.)[2] He boasts instead about how often he was beaten. He brags about rejection from his countrymen and his brushes with death. He lets people know that, as an apostle, he constantly faced imprisonment, hardship, sleeplessness, slander, and hunger. "Three times I was beaten with rods, once I was stoned, three times I was shipwrecked, a night and a day I have spent in the deep" (2 Cor 11:25).

Such a catalog stands in stark contrast to the popular idea of apostolic ministry at our celebrated conferences and grand green rooms. Many today actually establish their ministries on their *avoidance* of looking weak or foolish in the world's eyes. It is no wonder that the western church often lacks God's presence. If we are not willing for the cross' weakness, neither will we enjoy its power.

Not everyone is called to be an apostolic missionary like Paul. Not everyone is called to suffer the same ways he did. But the point of his hardships speaks to us amid our own troubles. *They loudly remind us that in ourselves we are weak, and we desperately need God.* It is called wisdom, therefore, to embrace the difficulties that make us feel and look weak. For they compel us to lean heavily on the Lord, and when we do that, we become strong in His strength. That is the wisdom of the cross.

To live by God's wisdom, then, we must accentuate our *weaknesses* to awaken our dependence on God. On the positive side of the equation, the cross' wisdom seeks to live deliberately by the *power* of the Holy Spirit. This is the great wisdom exchange: we bring our weakness to God by faith and trade it for His power. Yet this exchange is so uneven and contrary to human pride, that it seems like absolute madness to the natural mind.

Only the Holy Spirit can reveal God's unique wisdom to the human heart. Only the Holy Spirit can empower us to walk in that wisdom. The Holy Spirit is in fact the Spirit of wisdom (Isa 11:2; Eph 1:17; Col 1:9). When we actively cultivate life in the Spirit, we are living by the wisdom of the cross. The wealthy western church, including Pentecostals and Charismatics, must rediscover the person of the Holy Spirit as the same Spirit of *wisdom* by whom Jesus lived.

> He came to His hometown and began teaching them in their synagogue, so that they were astonished, and said, "Where did this man get this wisdom and these miraculous powers?" (Matt 13:54).

The world should be asking the church the same question. Where do they get such wisdom and miraculous powers? And the answer should be the same for us as it was for Jesus: we receive our wisdom and power from God, by His Spirit, in Jesus' name.

How else could Jesus shock the masses with teachings that crushed centuries of tradition? How else could He awaken corpses, liberate people tormented by spirits, or restore bodies poisoned by disease? *Only* through the Holy Spirit—dwelling in Him, hovering around Him, flowing from Him like a river.

How did Jesus stay focused on His traveling mission when conventional, human wisdom would have exploited His miracles, rescued Him from danger, and marketed Him as a political messiah? He could have gathered an army or ravaged His enemies through legions of warring angels. Instead, He submitted to His Father's plan, including rejection and death. As a result, Jesus saved the world and now rules forever. How did He conduct His life so perfectly *against* the grain of the world's wisdom and *with* the grain of God's wisdom?

By living His whole life through the person of the Holy Spirit, and allowing the Holy Spirit to live through Him.

God calls us to the same life of wisdom. Our weaknesses are cues for that life the Holy Spirit wants to live through us. So when we are caught on the horns of a dilemma, face a serious crisis, or endure the challenges of daily life, we do not need to fall back on the world's wisdom, resorting to the arm of the flesh through fear, anger, manipulation, complaining, tension, or playing the victim. We can instead pray in the Spirit and search the Scriptures till God's unique, cross-centered wisdom becomes clear for that situation. Then we can walk on the pathway of that wisdom. It may require us to remain silent under criticism, forgive wrongs, bless someone who hurt us, or pray in tongues for an hour. Any of these may look foolish to the world or to our natural souls. But they reflect the wisdom of the cross—the wisdom that powerfully bears fruit in God's kingdom.

Here is the wisdom of the cross: "'Not by might, nor by power, but by my Spirit,' says the Lord of hosts" (Zech 4:6). Once we have yielded our souls to the cross-shaped, Spirit-empowered wisdom of God, we are able to bear the marks described in the remaining chapters.

---

1. Michael Card, "God's Own Fool," *Scandalon*, Sparrow Records, 1986.
2. See 2 Cor 11:1, 16-17, 19, 21; 12:6, 11.

2

REST

The Value of Divine Rest

> Come to me, all of you who are weary and burdened, and I will give you rest (Matt 11:28, CSB).

Divine rest leaves a scar that signifies our death to the lusts of fear and striving and our resurrection to the Messiah's peaceful rule.

Hebrews tells us to be diligent to enter this rest (Heb 4:11). That means Sabbath rest is worth fighting for. In fact, it's worth dying for. Jesus died on Friday and rested on the Sabbath, awaiting His resurrection. As His body lay in the grave, Jesus was entering—and effecting—the ultimate rest from the works of the old creation. Likewise, spiritual Sabbath-rest requires a death to ourselves in many ways. That is why it leaves a scar, a mark of the cross.

True rest is one of the most precious treasures in God's Kingdom. It is the sign that we have believed, repented, and received the gift of salvation and that we enjoy the confidence of forgiven sins and a clean conscience.

> In repentance and rest you will be saved, in quietness and trust is your strength (Isa 30:15).
>
> Let us draw near to God with a sincere heart and with the full assurance that faith brings, having our hearts sprinkled to cleanse us from a guilty conscience (Heb 10:22, NIV).
>
> Therefore, having been justified by faith, we have peace with God through our Lord Jesus Christ (Rom 5:1).

Salvation puts us at peace with God. As a result, our hearts can rest from guilt, striving, and fear of judgment. When we are more conscious of the atonement of Jesus Christ than we are of our past sins, we enter the Sabbath Jesus died to give us. A truly clear conscience is a great source of confidence in all areas of life.

Rest also comes when we give our burdens to God in prayer. After He lifts heavy concerns from our hearts, He replaces them with His supernatural peace.

> Do not be anxious about anything, but in every situation, by prayer and petition, with thanksgiving, present your requests to God. And the peace of God, which transcends all understanding, will guard your hearts and your minds in Christ Jesus (Phil 4:6-7, NIV).

This verse promises a supernatural peace that defies circumstances and logic. It "transcends all understanding." It is the miraculous cure to anxiety. Worry can lead to deeper pain and foolish decisions. But the heart's peaceful rest in Jesus protects us from the stress that causes confusion. It allows us to think clearly and discern God's wisdom. It also makes room in our hearts for the joy of the Lord, enabling us to be confident even while facing serious problems. God's rest is powerful.

Indeed, God's rest is the place of spiritual victory. Entering divine Sabbath is like climbing a rock far above our enemies (Psa 61:2). Just getting on top of that rock—simply coming to a place of rest in our hearts—removes spiritual enemies from positions they were trying to occupy around us. That is why the Bible tells us to "let the peace of Christ rule in your hearts" (Col 3:15) and "the God of peace will soon crush Satan under your feet" (Rom 16:20). When we come to that place of peace, we have already overcome several enemies.

When facing a problem or attack, then, God's strategy is not always to start rebuking the devil. Sometimes it's not even His will to start praying about the immediate problem. Often the best thing to do is worship until we get a fresh vision of God for that situation. With that vision our hearts can rest, trusting all is well and He will bring us through. Then our faith is renewed—that "shield of faith, with which you can extinguish all the flaming darts of the evil one" (Eph 6:16, ESV).

Naturally there are times when the only way to unburden our hearts is to petition God about the immediate problem.

But the primary goal is always the same: *enter His rest*. From that place we overcome discouragement, walk in victory, and obtain courage to do whatever God requires (Phil 4:13). As Bill Johnson has said, "You have authority over any storm you can sleep in" (see Matt 8:23-27).

This is why the Bible tells us to "make every effort to enter that rest" (Heb 4:11, CSB). God's rest is so valuable that, if our hearts are not at peace, we must apply diligent energy in prayer to regain His rest. Remember what the old hymn says:

> *What a friend we have in Jesus, all our sins and griefs to bear.*
> *What a privilege to carry everything to God in prayer.*
> *O what peace we often forfeit, O what needless pain we bear,*
> *All because we do not carry everything to God in prayer.*[1]

No wonder God commanded Israel to keep the Sabbath. Among other things, it was a symbol of intimacy with Him that gives us rest in the middle of raging storms. He is then glorified through us as the source of real life and peace. So let's honor the Sabbath. Let's enter His rest. Let's come to Jesus whenever our hearts slip even slightly out of His peace.

The Secret to Entering God's Rest

There's more to this treasure of rest, so let's dig deeper. The secret to God's miraculous rest is found in one simple phrase…

Come to Me.

Jesus Himself is the secret to God's rest. He is the treasure buried beneath the sand of difficulties and doubts, formulas and fears. God's peace does not come as the result of solving a problem or removing a nuisance. His rest is divine, otherworldly, totally unique. We cannot get to it through human wisdom or by striving to fulfill religious obligations—praying enough, fasting enough, meditating enough, giving enough. His utterly unique rest is found in His utterly unique Son.

When we find Jesus, we find rest.

He is the pearl of great price. He is the treasure hidden in the field for which we joyfully sell everything, including useless anxieties, to buy that field.

However, the reason I call Jesus the "secret" to entering God's rest is not because He hides from us, but because we sometimes hide from Him. Too frequently the moment a storm arises, right when we need Him the most, our first instinct, strangely, is to turn somewhere else. But why? Why do we sometimes turn first to complaints or worry or cheap substitutes or religious recipes when God has offered Himself to us?

Maybe it's because we do not yet know Him as we ought to know Him. Maybe we haven't developed the kind of relationship that He has graciously made available to us. Oswald Chambers said, "Resting in the Lord does not depend on external circumstances at all, but on your relationship to God Himself."[2]

The first step, then, is simply to come. Again, Chambers said, "Anything that disturbs rest in Him must be cured at once, and it is not cured by being ignored, but by *coming to Jesus Christ*."[3] This takes loving determination. He requires diligence to enter His rest. So let's make our way to Him. Refuse the obstacles that distract you or seek to replace Him.

Be like the woman who was bleeding internally for twelve years, who "had suffered a great deal under the care of many doctors and had spent all she had, yet instead of getting better she grew worse" (Mark 5:26, NIV). Then, on the day Jesus was passing by, she had to contend with a large crowd pressing around Him.

But she dug her way through… through people, past failures, doubt, shame, and all other options. She had to touch Jesus; she had to experience *Him*. Probably on her hands and knees in the crowd, her arms reaching through the swarm of feet and legs and dirt, she grasped the edge of Jesus' cloak. At once she felt a silent, distinct jolt as divine life rushed into her and the bleeding stopped. Jesus said to her, "Daughter, your faith has saved you. Go in peace and be healed of your affliction" (Mark 5:34, CSB). She had gotten hold of Jesus. She entered His rest.

So can we. He's calling us now. *Come to Me.*

Come to Him, not just to lift the burden or solve the problem, but to know Him, to experience Him as He is. "Oh, taste and see that the Lord is good! Blessed is the man who takes refuge in Him!" (Psa 34:8, ESV). He is wonderful. He is gentle and humble of heart. His love and care are constant and comprehensive. When we grasp hold of Him, His life flows into ours. The glory of His character rubs off on us, transforms us, and rules our hearts with peace. Then the secret is unveiled: He becomes our rest.

Come to Me.

I believe the Lord is whispering this little phrase to His church. He burns for deep friendship with His people, a relationship that defines life itself for everyone who calls himself a Christian. Paul said that his very identity revolved around this one pursuit: "that I may know Him" (Phil 3:10). And his goal for the churches was the same: that "we all attain to the unity of the faith, and of the knowledge of the Son of God" (Eph 4:13).

Jesus said to His Father: "This is eternal life, that they may know You, the only true God, and Jesus Christ whom You have sent" (John 17:3). His call to the church is simply to come to Him, discover more of who He is, and walk out that knowledge in daily life.

So it's worth doing a heart-check once in a while. It's worth asking some honest questions about the content of our lives. Are we really increasing in the knowledge of Jesus Christ? Is every area of our lives focused on the single pursuit of knowing Him? Or are we just getting by as good Christians?

Pastors and leaders should ask similar questions about their churches. Is our church maturing in the knowledge of Jesus Christ? Or are we focused more on programs that attract people to our building and services? Are my teachings or sermons *unveiling Him* to those listening? Or am I only preparing sermons and meeting the demands of people? Are church members demonstrably becoming more like Jesus? Or are they merely attending?

All the while He continues to call. Come… to…

Me.

I am convinced we must discover afresh the wonderful person of Jesus Christ. That on-going discovery is the key to revival, evangelism, church planting, discipleship, and maturity in the church. The beauty of Jesus Christ blinds us, as it did Saul of Tarsus, to the deceptive charm of things less valuable.

> *No angel in the sky, can fully bear that sight,*
> *But downward bends his burning eye, at*
> *mysteries so bright.*[4]

The sheer magnitude of His persona is the substance behind "Me" when He says, "Come to Me." He is fully God, and He is fully human—the perfect, pure, and utterly unique fusion of divinity and humanity. He is both transcendent and down-to-earth. At His core He is love. In His character He is good. In His one, eternal person, He elegantly blends affection, mercy, grace, and kindness with truth, holiness, justice, and power.

The spiritually dry soul does not need more of this world's temporary satisfactions. The church longing for revival does not need more human wisdom on how to be successful. *We need a fresh revelation of the glory of Jesus Christ.* We need the river of God's Spirit to flood our hearts again, "resulting in a true knowledge of God's mystery, that is, Christ Himself" (Col 2:2). If you are dry or longing for revival, seek Him. Make it your ambition to discover Him a little more each day. You won't be disappointed.

Paul rightly said, "Christ is all" (Col 3:11). He is all that God is and all that human hearts need. For the sinner, He is Savior. For the sick, He is Healer. To the thirsty, He is the source of Living Water. To the hungry, He is True Bread from heaven. To those in darkness, He is the Light of the world. And to those in the tomb, He is the Resurrection and the Life.

Theologians find that "in Him all the fullness of deity dwells in bodily form" (Col 2:9). Philosophers discern that "in Him are hidden all the treasures of wisdom and knowledge" (Col 2:3). Scientists discover that "in Him all things hold together" (Col 1:17).

He is the poor man's Treasure and the rich man's Master. He is the Teacher of disciples and the Playmate of children. For Jews He is Messiah-King. For Gentiles He is Lord of all. At the dawn of creation He was Alpha; at the end of history He is Omega. Christ is all.

Christ is all.

It is no wonder, then, that Paul described the heart and soul of his ministry by saying, "We proclaim Him" (Col 1:28). It is time to rediscover Jesus in our lives, families, churches, and ministries. He's saying to us now, "Come to Me." When we do, we experience Him who is Sabbath, the place of rest from which we can do all things.

1. Joseph Medlicott Scriven, *What a Friend We Have in Jesus* (1855), https://hymnary.org/text/what_a_friend_we_have_in_jesus_all_our_s.
2. Oswald Chambers, *My Utmost for His Highest* (New York: Dodd, Mead & Company, 1935, 1963) 186 (July 4th entry).
3. Ibid. 232 (Aug 19 entry); emphasis added.
4. Matthew Bridges and Godfrey Thring, *Crown Him with Many Crowns* (1851), https://www.jubilate.co.uk/songs/crown_him_with_many_crowns_jubilate_version.

3

MEEKNESS

The cross is the ultimate expression of Jesus' selfless love. It is the kind of love through which royalty expresses its essential nature. In God's Kingdom, kings carry crosses. And I believe that no character trait reveals the majesty of the cross more than meekness. Meekness is an essential mark of the cross. It is the ongoing death of self, leaving the deepest scar on the soul.

Meekness is a facet of humility. The New Testament Greek word, *prautēs*, can mean gentleness, humility, friendliness, or even courtesy. The English term comes from a word meaning soft or gentle and is often associated with weakness. But biblical meekness, the meekness of Jesus Christ, is not rooted in weakness. It is rooted in power.

True meekness emerges from that cluster of character traits belonging to people who thrive in the Holy Spirit. They live from the divine life abiding inside, not in reaction to the pressures and provocations swarming outside. Their hearts are in order, even if the world around them is not. They can sleep on the boat while the storm rages, for the peace of Christ is ruling in their hearts (Col 3:15). Death itself has been defeated by their Lord. God's peace-making dominion is more real to them than the chaos trying to destroy their security.

Those who are truly meek value the expansion of God's Kingdom more than anything—more than reputation, financial success, or earthly well-being. Nothing, therefore, can threaten them. And if they cannot be threatened, they will not react with fear or anger when assailed. Instead, they will respond to every attack with gentleness, remaining at rest in the impregnable rock of surrender.

Meekness is the offspring of rest.

How, then, do we find such rest in a chaotic world? We rest when we entrust our souls to God. That means we do not belong to ourselves; God possesses us: our bodies, families, jobs, present, and future. Our complete inheritance is safe with Him.

"Happy are the meek, for *they will inherit* the earth" (Matt 5:5, my translation and emphasis).

Which means we're off the hook. If we believe the King's promises, no one can steal our birthright or trick us out of our inheritance. We cannot be robbed of our destiny. We trust that God is "able to guard what [we] have entrusted to Him until that day" (2 Tim 1:12). Therefore, *we can afford to be meek.* There's no demand to compete against people. We have no need to insist on our rights or fight others for our territory. God will grant us that. We are liberated, free to be gentle even when others oppose us, take from us, or succeed instead of us.

> Wait and trust the Lord. Don't be upset when others get rich or when someone else's plans succeed. Don't get angry. Don't be upset; it only leads to trouble. Evil people will be sent away, but those who trust the Lord will inherit the land. In a little while the wicked will be no more. You may look for them, but they will be gone. People who are not proud will inherit the land and will enjoy complete peace (Psa 37:7-11, NCV).

May the King's meekness mark His people and create a gentle revolution in the earth.

Jesus, Model of Meekness

> Come to Me, all those toiling and overloaded, and I Myself will give you rest. Take My yoke on you and learn from Me, because I am meek and humble in heart, and you will find rest for your souls. For My yoke is easy and My load is light (Matt 11:28-30, my translation).

Meekness is one of the most fundamental character traits of Jesus Christ. In fact, in some ways, I believe it is His central character trait. I say this for two reasons.

First, meekness typically expresses itself through gentleness, and Jesus was the gentlest man who ever lived. Even under the fire of criticism, Jesus did not quarrel with His enemies to defend Himself. He often refrained from personal conflict in order to touch the lives of the afflicted, just as the Scriptures declared the Messiah would do. "He will not quarrel, nor cry out; nor will anyone hear His voice in the streets. A battered reed He will not break off, and a smoldering wick He will not put out" (Matt 12:19-20).

Though Jesus was perfectly holy, He did not intimidate or repulse sinners; He welcomed them. He ate meals with them and enjoyed their company. With respect and love, He valued them as those made in God's image. Though He possessed the power to destroy the rebellious human race, He chose to come among them as one of them, kindly and tenderly, to heal and forgive them. That is gentleness. There has been no gentler person in all of history than Jesus Christ.

But second, Jesus' meekness produced much more than a gentle demeanor. Gentle behavior comes from meekness. It is one brook that flows from the vast river-source of meekness. But it is not itself meekness. Rather, meekness flowed from the deep of Jesus' character, encompassing His other attributes. This is why we read gospel stories in which Jesus, the gentle Healer, did not always act with mild manners.

Jesus physically wrecked the operation of the temple marketeers for defiling God's house of prayer (Mark 11:15-17). He confronted the Pharisees with anger for elevating traditional Sabbath rules over human need (Mark 3:1-6) and passionately condemned them for their duplicity. He decried them as hypocrites, stung them with woes, and publicly announced their crimes (Matt 23). Jesus even rebuked one of his closest friends, calling Peter "Satan" when he sought to put a stumbling block across Jesus' path to redemptive suffering (Mark 8:33).

These actions are not gentle in the conventional sense of the word. They are passionate, compelling, fearless…

But not gentle.

So if the Model of Meekness could shift into a mode of such strong, incendiary actions and words, what then is meekness? What is that deeper, divine quality that handles a fragile soul with the tender warmth of a nursing mother, yet can rage against religious opposition with the blazing fire of holy wrath?

True meekness is the condition of character that has absolutely no agenda—except for God's.

Jesus was meek because He came to earth with no plans of His own, no mission except the one God gave Him. He had no personal ambition, no private scheme to promote or protect, no need to watch over His reputation. Jesus did not seek a Holy Grail that promised personal fulfillment while derailing Him from His God-given mission (Matt 4:1-11).

In fact, He found *no* satisfaction in this present age. "I have food to eat that you do not know about" (John 4:32). Only Father's mission filled the craving in Jesus' mighty heart. "My food is to do the will of Him who sent Me and to accomplish His work" (John 4:34).

That is meekness. It says, "Your kingdom come, Your will be done at whatever cost necessary to Me. Nothing else satisfies. Every other consideration is dead. I have nothing to possess or gain in this world except Your will." No one could steal that from Jesus; no one could threaten Him. His well-being and identity were determined, and sheltered, by His meekness.

Liberated from the demands of people's opinions, both flatterers and foes, Jesus literally had nothing to lose. Therefore, He was always completely at the Father's disposal.

None of the special interest groups of Israel could prevail upon Him to join their cause, or even support them. No Pharisee could convert Him to their puritan movement. No Sadducee could pressure Him into temple politics. No Zealot could recruit Him into militant nationalism. Not even Judas' betrayal could tempt Him to defend His honor.

He never had to calculate His words to maintain popular opinion. He never feared the cost of obedience. As a result, He could hear the Spirit's faintest whispers and feel the subtlest promptings. Having no self-interest or commitment to self-preservation, Jesus was acutely sensitive to the will of the One with whom he had to do. And that precisely was His meekness. Jesus was the Model of Meekness.

All hail this Model of Meekness! He is the King of Glory! Happy are all who follow Him. They are liberated by the laying down of their rights for the sake of a higher call. They may possess nothing in this age, but one day they will inherit the earth.

Keep Coming to Jesus

When Jesus calls the exhausted and overloaded to Himself, He is inviting us to rest inside His sanctuary of meekness. But there's more to His invitation than finding respite from chaos. Jesus is calling us, not just to shelter us, but to transform us into His image. True discipleship is all about becoming like Jesus. So when Jesus says, "Come to Me… I am meek...," He specifically calls us to a core attribute that encompasses so many others. He is calling us to embrace and reflect His meekness.

Jesus is the Model of Meekness, and the call to follow His example of meekness hinges on two practical commands: "Come to Me" and "Learn from Me."

Jesus' call to come to Him is rooted in the soil of the Old Testament prophets. It is the updated version of their ancient but essential message. When Jesus beckons us to come, like the prophets before Him, He is summoning us to repent. But remember: repentance in God's Kingdom is more than a turning away from sin; it is a turning *to God*. True repentance does more than break old habits and start new ones. Repentance very specifically embraces God and His ways. It trades self-centered living for the Lord himself: knowing Him, being with Him, learning from Him, and obeying Him.

So when the prophets called wayward Israel to turn from their idols, it was always so they could return to God Himself. Breaking covenant with Him was the root crime. Repairing that covenant was root repentance. Likewise, in our context, Jesus calls people directly to Himself. He is the One to whom the prophets always pointed. Jesus is the Lord; therefore, He says, "Come to *Me*."

The prophets also promised that, when Israel did return to the Lord, they would be refreshed by His presence. Whatever pain, sorrow, or trouble they were experiencing because of their sins, the Lord would wash it all away. He would deliver them from the consequences of their rebellion; He would heal them of self-inflicted wounds; He would revive them out of spiritual despondency. The demand for repentance was always coupled with an invitation to revival.

> Ho! Everyone who thirsts, come to the waters, and you who have no money come, buy and eat. Come, buy wine and milk without money and without cost. Why do you spend money for what is not bread, and your wages for what does not satisfy? Listen carefully to Me, and eat what is good, and delight yourself in abundance. Incline your ear and *come to Me*. Listen, that you may live, and I will make an everlasting covenant with you, according to the faithful mercies shown to David (Isa 55:1-3, emphasis added).
>
> Stand by the ways and see and ask for the ancient paths, where the good way is, and walk in it; and *you will find rest for your souls*... (Jer 6:16, emphasis added).

Jesus' call to come to Him and find rest issues from the tradition of these prophets. But there is one major difference. The prophets called people to the Lord who was speaking through them. Jesus calls people to Himself. He *is* the Lord to whom we repent and from whom we drink the refreshing waters of revival.

The first step, then, for us to follow Jesus as the Model of Meekness, is to repent in the true, biblical sense of the term. We must turn away from our sins, idols, and other sources of selfish satisfaction and come to Jesus Himself. Whether we have strayed from Him completely or have wandered off in certain areas, He calls us to return.

But the Lord's call to us is not just for when we stray. He *always* says, "Come to Me"—every chance we get, at every turn of our path. Coming to Jesus is a way of life. People often enter valleys, or face serious problems, without really, deeply turning to Him for peace and wisdom. Jesus' solution is simple. No matter what the situation, no matter what the season, He continually says, *Come to Me*.

Meekness, then, is a life fully yielded to Jesus. It begins with repentance and continues as a lifestyle that constantly comes out of the chaos, confusion, and complications of life... *to Him*. Like a lighthouse in the middle of raging seas, Jesus constantly radiates His welcoming command, "Come to Me." Those who heed that command learn what meekness really is.

Learn from Jesus

Jesus' call is not just to come to Him; it is also to learn from Him. The essence of discipleship is learning the ways of the Master and walking in those ways. In fact, Jesus' call to come and learn is a forecast to the Great Commission at the end of Matthew's gospel (Matt 28:18-20). There Jesus says to make disciples by baptizing new believers, then teaching them to obey everything He commanded them. Here in a miniature commission (Matt 11:28-30), He says something similar, inviting people to come to Him so they can learn from Him.

While the Great Commission instructs Jesus' disciples to teach all He commanded, this earlier version tells disciples specifically to learn His meekness. This is because meekness is an essential component to Jesus' total character. If we possess the Lord's meekness, we have the power to perform His commands. For meekness is the absence of personal agenda and is therefore foundational to the obedience Jesus requires.

If we lack this foundation of meekness, how can we obey all of the Lord's other commands? They would require too much from us. Without meekness, we are still trying to hold on to our own reputation or ambitions. How, then, can we afford to offer the other cheek after being slapped? Or forgive relentlessly? Or continue to love those who persecute or betray us?

Without the meekness of Jesus coursing through our veins, these responses, and others like them, are impossible. We cannot afford His selfless, crucified lifestyle if we have not already settled the issue that we don't belong to ourselves. Our lives must be like Jesus' life: at God's disposal in every way, at all times. That is meekness. It is the cross made practical, and it activates God's power to obey all of His commands.

Meekness is the way Jesus exercised His royalty and took dominion over His enemies.[1] That means we too must intentionally learn from Jesus how to be meek. How can we do that?

Take up His yoke

A yoke was a wooden frame that either joined together two animals to pull a load or allowed a person to carry two heavy objects across his shoulders. The Jews used it as a symbol of dedication and obedience to the Torah. Studying and obeying the Law was the way they expressed their devotion to God as Master, as well as their responsibility to carry His commands in the world. But here Jesus uses it as a symbol of exclusive devotion to Him and His teachings.

Jesus calls us to make a fundamental decision to bow to His yoke alone. That means we have made Him our only option. Learning from Jesus is not done on our terms, but on His terms. So we begin our learning process by resolving deeply in our hearts that we are devoted to Jesus—His ways and His teachings—not to ourselves or anyone else. His manner of life becomes our personal culture. He is our Master; we are His disciples. Then we find that His yoke is liberating, inspiring, and eternally satisfying. Life becomes utter joy. *His yoke is easy.*

Learn from Him

The Greek words for "learn" (*manthanō*) and "disciple" (*mathētēs*) share the same root. This tells us that *disciples learn.* They are devoted protégés that have come to know Jesus Christ as Life itself, and have therefore committed themselves to the lifelong endeavor of learning His virtues and assimilating them into their souls. Disciples have caught sight of Jesus' eternal value and cannot look away. "Lord, to whom shall we go? You have the words of eternal life" (John 6:68, LEB).

Now entrapped by love and the words of the coming age, they pursue Him: "Rabbi (which translated means Teacher), where are you staying?" And He responds: "Come, and you will see" (John 1:38-39). Then they abide with Him to watch His lifestyle and listen to His teaching. They follow Him and sit at His feet and unearth the treasures of His meekness and humility. Anyone in the crowd can have an encounter with Jesus during the excitement of revival. But disciples surrender to His yoke and learn the traits of meekness and humility.

Notice that, just prior to His invitation to come and learn, Jesus "began to denounce the cities in which most of His miracles were done, because they did not repent" (Matt 11:20). These cities encountered Jesus in ways others had only dreamed of. They experienced His glory, beholding great signs and wonders. But they did not want to see the priceless treasures of meekness to which those signs pointed. If they did, they would have become disciples—loyal learners of the meekness that qualified this Man to be King of the Universe.

People tend to desire the benefits of power without the sacrifices of character. God wants both. So when Jesus comes to town, He's looking for something specific. He may visit our cities and blow us away with miracles. But as electrifying as these visitations are, the Master Fisherman is looking into the deep waters. He scans the crowd. His X-ray eyes dart to and fro, looking to support those whose hearts are completely His. Jesus is always searching for disciples, for sons and daughters of peace who will invite Him into their homes. When He sees such people, the Lord bids them come to learn His ways.

True repentance does not merely walk to the front of a building and say a prayer to "receive salvation." True repentance yokes itself to Jesus forever and says, "Teach me, O Lord, the way of Your statutes, and I shall keep it to the end" (Psa 119:33, NKJV). Jesus calls us to Himself to learn His meekness. How do we do this today?

Through the Word. Specifically, we must rediscover Jesus in the four gospels and see Him there with fresh eyes. These divinely-inspired biographies, full of the simple but extraordinary stories and sayings of Jesus, beckon us to behold a Man like no other. They call us, not merely to read them, but to feast on them, devouring the essence of their unusual Hero into our spirits. And that essence is divine, eternal meekness, enshrined in the flesh of authentic humanity and recounted for us in words too simple to be misunderstood and too wonderful to be ignored—words that describe the Indescribable. As one author said, "If Jesus had never lived, we would not be able to invent him."[2] True meekness cannot be found in any books of philosophy or history. It can only be found in the Spirit-inspired Scriptures that describe Jesus, the Model of Meekness.

The four gospels give four accounts of the One who could never, ever have been contrived by human ingenuity. No eye has seen and no ear has heard. For "never has a man spoken the way this man speaks" (John 7:46). He fits into no existing, earthly categories; He rather comes to us in His own, pre-existing category, and then stands in it by Himself. Yet the Holy Spirit has seen to it that we would have access to the very books that paint the portrait of this unimaginable Figure. What a privilege to have such writings—to possess the stories and teachings that unveil the divinely meek King —that we might learn His ways.

Unlike the gods of ancient Greek myths, or the lead characters in modern movies, the Jesus of the gospels refuses to overpower His enemies with selfish, carnal vengeance or prove Himself through temporal force—either through physical violence or verbal attack. Instead, He entrusts

Himself to God and refuses to defend or promote Himself. He proclaims the gospel with boldness. He eats with sinners. He feeds multitudes. He serves the poor. He performs miracles, teaches, and heals. And in the end, instead of conquering His enemies by calling on His Father for twelve legions of angels, He lays down His life out of love. Then God vindicates Him by raising Him from the dead. That is meekness, and the cross stands at its center.

Yet none of this negates the glorious, sobering reality of the Day of the Lord, "When the Lord Jesus will be revealed from heaven with His mighty angels in flaming fire, dealing out retribution to those who do not know God and to those who do not obey the gospel of our Lord Jesus" (2 Thess 1:7-8). Both aspects are true and necessary—the Lamb and the Lion—because both express the Lord's meekness. In this world, and during this age, Judah's Lion would not conquer as the world would conquer. He would conquer only as a Lamb. This was the Father's way—the only way to dislodge the enemy's foothold in sin and death. It was ingrained too deeply in the human soul and spread too broadly throughout creation. We needed the Lamb who was slain to shed the only blood able to cleanse our filthy garments. But just as our salvation is rooted in the slain Lamb, so is the Day of the Lord. Both radiate the same meekness.

Only Jesus could embody perfect meekness. The same lamb-like Servant, "Who will not break off a battered reed nor put out a smoldering wick," will also one day "lead justice to victory" (Matt 12:19-20). "In Your majesty ride on victoriously, for the cause of truth and meekness and righteousness" (Psa 45:4). Meekness looks like a Lamb in this age. But the same meekness comes to judge like a Lion at the end. From a human point of view, this union of gentleness and holy vengeance in one meekness is a paradox. But from a divine point of view, there is no other way a Lamb can be a Lamb without also being a Lion—and vice versa.

> The LORD, the LORD, a God merciful and gracious, slow to anger, and abounding in steadfast love and faithfulness, keeping steadfast love for thousands, forgiving iniquity and transgression and sin, but who will by no means clear the guilty, visiting the iniquity of the fathers on the children and the children's children, to the third and the fourth generation (Exod 34:6-7, ESV).

> Behold, the lion of the tribe of Judah, the root of David, has conquered, so that he can open the scroll and its seven seals. And I saw in the midst of the throne and of the four living creatures and in the midst of the elders a Lamb... (Rev 5:5-6, LEB).

It is impossible to replicate divine meekness in our own power. How can we possibly become reproductions of this indescribable Model of Meekness? Only by learning His meekness from the sacred writings that describe Him, and allowing His Spirit to formulate that same character in us.

We must get the living Word of such meekness into our souls to replace our tendency toward mere human justice on our terms. We must leave room for God's wrath in the future by overcoming evil with good in the present (Rom 12:19-21). Jesus conquered through meekness, becoming the Model of Meekness for us. So must we read, study, and memorize—indeed, we must bask and soak—in the Jesus story of the gospels. He is calling us to learn His meekness through the Word.

Through Prayer. When Jesus first said, "Come to Me," He knew His words would reverberate into every generation as a call to commune with Him in prayer. One of the trillions of echoes of that resonance made its way into the book you now read. In fact, their sound may be striking your heart afresh—at this very moment—in a way tailored just for you. The Lord may now be calling you to a kind of prayer that connects with Him on a deeper level and for greater transformation. But the sound of the invitation is quite specific. It does not merely say, "Come to Me and rest." It says, "Come to Me and rest by learning My meekness." This is a call to prayerful discipleship and disciple-making prayer.

We often come to Jesus out of desperate need. We seek refuge in Him because we are toiled and overloaded. In ourselves we are indeed frail. Our motivations for racing into His arms span the spectrum of human emotions in a troubled world. This age constantly seeks to stress us out, unwittingly helping us realize how much we need rest in Jesus. He is our refuge and strength, a very present help in time of trouble. Such prayer is right, good, and essential; we must do it often. But we must also remember that our refuge is also our Teacher. We must come to Him for help and safety, but we must also come to Him to learn.

That rest we seek in the presence of the Lord will settle more deeply and permanently when we come to Him intentionally to learn His meekness. Or to put it in Paul's words, prayer that comes to learn from Jesus is prayer that comes to behold His glory for the express purpose of being transformed into the same image. Jesus, the Word become flesh who tabernacled among His disciples in Israel, is now present by the Spirit. To *come* to Jesus is to *behold* His glory. And to *learn* from Jesus is to be *transformed* by that glory.

> But we all, with unveiled face, beholding as in a mirror the glory of the Lord, are being transformed into the same image from glory to glory, just as from the Lord, the Spirit (2 Cor 3:18).

When we connect with His glory for the sake of transformation, that is the moment Jesus says, "You will find rest for your souls." His glory melts us into the meekness of Jesus Christ. And that meekness leads us into more and more of the land of Sabbath rest.

Take a moment and ponder this familiar word in a fresh way. Do not allow "glory" to fall the way of cliché. Glory refers to the Lord's luminous Presence—the weighty, new covenant manifestation of His Spirit, the very Being of God Himself, sacred, indescribable, eternal, and awesome—given to us so we can behold Him and be transformed into His image. Glory is not static; it is dynamic. It does not merely hover as a spectacle; it radiates divinity as creative power. It transforms us.

The Lord's glory is His heavenly beauty, the copious emanation of His dazzling, divine virtues that, when beheld, strikes us as so utterly awesome, winsome, and desirable, that we must do more than feel it. We must engage it and become *like* it. The Lord's glory expresses the outward radiance of His inward virtue, it exhales His fragrant affections and stamps His holy character onto our hearts to reshape them into His likeness. To behold Jesus Christ's meekness with the eyes of our hearts wide open in awe and adoration, is to drink that meekness visually into our souls. The glory of meekness demands we do more than offer petitions; it demands we behold and become.

To change the metaphor: the prayer that seeks to *learn* Jesus' meekness is the prayer that seeks to *feast* on His virtues. So Jesus' metaphor of yoking is parallel to Paul's metaphor of beholding. Now Paul's metaphor of beholding is parallel to David's metaphor of banqueting (Psa 23:5-6). Israel's sweet psalmist and warrior king imagined Yahweh's attributes as a table full of paradisiacal delights for the famished soul—a buffet of fruits and nuts and meats and wine spread before a weary pilgrim. "O taste and see that the Lord is good" (Psa 34:8). The imagery beckons us to contemplate the fruit of the Spirit as a spiritual banquet. Yes, we should *bear* the Spirit's fruit in our lives, but we should also *feast* on the Spirit's fruit in prayer. God's virtues have exquisite taste to the palate of our souls. And remember, "you are what you eat."

Let us delight in the edible fare of the Lord's glory. Behold the banquet of "love, joy, peace, patience, kindness, goodness, faithfulness, gentleness, and self-control" (Gal 5:22-23). What law condemns the worshipper who is so elated by the divine Personality that he does more than sing or petition or meditate, but he feasts on the Lord to become like Him? The ingestion of these divine attributes will then organically grow out of the life of the one who sits at the Lord's table in the temple. And of course, the word "gentleness" in the list above is the same word translated as "meekness" (*prautēs*). It belongs to the cornucopia of attributes we engage as a meal in worship and eventually show forth as character. Against such things there is no law.

When we become angry with a co-worker or church member who offended us, we turn to Jesus. There we learn from Him, behold Him, and we feast on His virtues. He speaks to us, He imparts His Spirit to us, and we sense His attitude toward that person. He is not fuming with offense, lusting to give that person a piece of His mind. Rather, He longs to have mercy and forgive. Yes, we may need to confront the person, or even remove a speck from his eye. But the Lord also sees the value and potential of that person, feels compassion, and will therefore approach the speck with gentle precision to remove it without harming the eyeball's delicate tissue.

When we turn to our Lord's presence in situations like these, His nature rubs off on us. Jesus teaches us His ways when we simply come to Him as He is, in His meekness. Once in His presence, free from the demands of selfish justice, ambition, religious pride, and worry, we learn His meekness and thereby enter His rest. His yoke is the easiest yoke to carry. From that place of rest, we can do anything.

---

1. See Psa 45:4; Matt 12:18-21; 21:5; 26:47-68.
2. Walter Wink, *The Powers That Be: Theology for a New Millennium* (New York: Doubleday, 1998) 81.

4
HUMILITY

The Secret of "Therefore"

> Therefore God exalted him to the highest place, and gave him the name that is above every name (Phil 2:9, NIV).

This extraordinary statement declares that Jesus is the Lord of heaven, earth, and all they contain.

When the verse says, "exalted Him to the highest place," the Greek verb (*hyperupsoō*) literally states that God "hyper-exalted" Jesus. That means God raised Him far above every creature. There is no higher authority than Jesus Christ—no dictator, president, monarch, or prime minister, and there is no greater power—no weapon, military, government, or demon. He is the incomparable, unrivaled, supreme Sovereign over all creation.

Marks of the Cross

The Bible takes this one step further when it declares that Jesus shares the benefits of His royalty with His people. God "appointed him to be head over everything *for the church*" (Eph 1:22, NIV, emphasis added). Christ's triumph over sin becomes our free gift when we believe. And His ongoing dominion over sin fuels our lifestyle of victory when we walk by faith.

But how do we put His awesome dominion into practice for daily life? The secret is in the "therefore."

The text above says, *therefore* God exalted Jesus. God did not elevate Him out of a vacuum. There was a specific reason God lifted Jesus on high and set Him in the premier place of all creation. So whatever comes before "therefore" is the reason God enthroned Christ. It is also our key to putting that dominion into daily practice.

Here is what Paul says before the "therefore":

> [Christ] made himself nothing by taking the very nature of a servant, being made in human likeness. And being found in appearance as a man, he humbled himself by becoming obedient to death—even death on a cross! *Therefore* God highly exalted him… (Phil 2:7-9, NIV, emphasis added).

God exalted His Son to the highest place *because His Son humbled Himself to the lowest place*. There is a direct correspondence between the two contrasting actions. The Son went down; the Father lifted Him up. Jesus is King of creation and Savior of all because He voluntarily surrendered Himself to His Father's will. He lowered Himself to the station of a servant, the form of a human, the obedience of a slave, and the death of a criminal. His horrible execution, marked by all the shame and torture that comes with Roman crucifixion, was the lowest possible place to which Jesus could have descended.

Such a descent is unthinkable for the holy Son of God who was perfectly divine and had done no wrong. But that was the only way we could be saved. Jesus lowered Himself as our servant, stooping into the humblest of circumstances. And that is why God exalted Him to the highest place in creation. This pattern reflects God's nature and the way of His Kingdom.

"Whoever exalts himself will be humbled, and whoever humbles himself will be exalted" (Matt 23:12, ESV). Jesus taught this principle, and He modeled it. The way up is down. A great tree begins with a buried seed. God exalted His Son, not because He insisted on His well-deserved greatness, but because He was willing to bury His rights and serve others. This is the Kingdom way.

That same "therefore" now teaches us how to walk Christ's victory out in daily life. To be saved we must only believe; it is a free gift. But to enjoy the ongoing practical benefits of Jesus' dominion in every area of life, we must walk as He walked. We must be willing to travel the same path of humility and generous service without trying to exalt ourselves or promote our own agenda. Our job is to carry our cross; His job is to exalt us at the proper time.

In other words, if we want to enjoy the King's dominion, we must embrace the King's character. And the character of our King is rooted in selfless love and sacrifice. As I said before, in God's Kingdom, kings carry crosses. "If anyone wishes to come after Me, he must deny himself, and take up his cross daily and follow Me. For whoever wishes to save his life will lose it, but whoever loses his life for My sake, he is the one who will save it" (Luke 9:23-24).

The cross was more than a one-time event for Jesus. It was His lifestyle—a personal culture that revealed the character of a true King. If we want the practical power of Jesus' resurrection, we must embrace the practical wisdom of His cross. Humility leads to greatness. Humility *is* greatness. "He has brought down rulers from their thrones, and has exalted those who were humble" (Luke 1:62). "Humble yourselves in the presence of the Lord, and He will exalt you" (James 4:10). The Kingdom pattern remains the same. Lambs sit on thrones, crowned with many crowns.

Human hearts crave greatness, but they do not naturally crave God's *way* to greatness. Jesus taught us to deny the inclination to exalt ourselves. He instructs us to trust God that, if we lower ourselves, He will exalt us. Such denial will leave a scar on our soul; for humility is one of the marks of the cross. But like Jesus, we will bear that mark in glory.

Let's look again at Jesus' call to come to Him. Just as it reveals His meekness, so does it reveal His humility.

> Come to Me, all those toiling and overloaded, and I Myself will give you rest. Take My yoke on you and learn from Me, because I am meek and humble in heart, and you will find rest for your souls. For My yoke is easy and My load is light (Matt 11:28-30, my translation).

Here Jesus declares the essence of humility. It is not the trumpeting of good works to look devout, but neither is it a preoccupied self-hatred. Jesus models humility in this passage by freely and completely *offering Himself for the restoration of others*. Humility is servanthood, but servanthood with a goal: to help others find the refreshing presence of the King.

Though He is God's royal Son, Jesus does not live for Himself. He does not come into the world demanding that people serve His needs or interests. He does not promote a selfish agenda, ordering people about and forcing them to confess loyalty to His Kingdom. Though He deserves loyalty and glory, and though His faithful subjects happily give Him what He deserves, He does not demand it or insist others recognize Him in a coerced, superficial way.

Instead, He first makes Himself available to serve the needs of others. He gently offers Himself as the source of life for any who would heed His call. And He never complains that no one recognizes the great sacrifice He makes to help us. He simply says, "Come; I am here for you. I understand the heavy burdens you carry. I will replace them with my lifestyle of divine rest and teach you how to live the same way. You can be carefree like a child forever."

Notice also that Jesus says He is humble *in heart*. This means that He does not fake humility, nor does He force Himself to help us despite His real irritation with us. Jesus is a humble person at His core, in the essential fabric of His personality. He really cares about us and desires to put our needs above His own. Jesus is quite content to lay His reputation aside in order to see others flourish in His Kingdom.

That way of life is very natural for Him because He is humble *in His heart*.

As a result of His sincere humility, Jesus can offer us the truest kind of rest: total restoration as humans who bear God's glorious image. People live under the tyranny of sin, demonic powers, death, sickness, poverty, depression, and abuse. Jesus proposes to deliver us from these spiritual despots and replace them with His exclusive yoke of leadership. His yoke, however, is not another burden. He does not intend to take away one form of oppression and replace it with another. No, His yoke is easy and His burden is light. He is not like the tyrants of our age. Jesus rules gently. He liberates. He *restores* us to become the kind of humans God designed us to be. He is like no Master in all of history or the entire Universe. To be ruled by Jesus is to enjoy the truest kind of freedom and peace.

That is why Jesus invites us to learn this same culture of humility for ourselves. In fact, that is the source of our continued rest. King Jesus first gives us rest by removing the oppression of evil from our lives. But the continued experience of rest comes when we learn to conduct ourselves with the same humility as our Master. Jesus essentially declares to us: "Learn from Me as the Humble One. When you follow Me and give up the burden of putting yourself forward, or putting your needs before others, you will find out how to live without care, pressure, and stress. That is My secret. My humble service to others is what keeps Me free from the exhausting reign of selfishness. If you put yourself under My tutelage, I will teach you that kind of humility. You will enter My rest, and you will help others enter My rest."

Jesus, the Hero of Humility

We live in a self-centered world. It's not easy to find heroes who shine simply because of their sacrificial service to God and others. The present political climate naturally ignores true, gospel-centered servitude. Popular media and society venerate celebrities who excel in the worlds of entertainment, sports, or business without necessarily any thought to their character. Or when the world does extol their character, it often does so on the basis of its own godless code of morality and justice, rather than God's Word. Then the images of these stars march ever before us on digital screens. People gaze upon them, adoring their charm, absorbing their values, and emulating their lifestyle. They are the heroes of this age.

We conform to the images we most intensely behold. And our culture does not look to figures who surrender to God and sacrificially serve others in Jesus' name. It does not cherish those who lower themselves under His dominion to lift others up. It values instead the self-made, the powerful, the independent, and the successful. Or it values those who serve their own agenda rather than God's. Genuine humility is thin on the ground in the new millennium of self-absorption and moral relativity.

This is why it is hard sometimes to find the qualities of real humility even among believers. Church is often a place for Christians to attend a concert, put their kids in a class, hear a good speaker, and perhaps socialize a bit, rather than to gather as spiritual family, behold Jesus Christ, and serve one another through the Spirit to become like Him. In other words, sadly, some believers are more influenced by the heroes of the world rather than the Hero at the center of their professed faith.

It's time to change our gaze. It's time to exchange heroes. It's time to transfer the Lord of glory from the pedestal of religious icon and put Him back on the actual throne of our minds, lifestyles, and churches. Let's make Jesus Christ our Hero again. Let's allow His humble character to become our way of life. If we want to walk in the humility of the cross, we must take a good, honest look at the Champion of the cross. We must behold the Lamb.

> Do nothing out of selfish ambition or vain conceit. Rather, in humility value others above yourselves, not looking to your own interests but each of you to the interests of the others. In your relationships with one another, have the same mindset as Christ Jesus: Who, being in very nature God, did not consider equality with God something to be used to his own advantage; rather, he made himself nothing by taking the very nature of a servant, being made in human likeness. And being found in appearance as a man, he humbled himself by becoming obedient to death—even death on a cross! Therefore God exalted him to the highest place and gave him the name that is above every name, that at the name of Jesus every knee should bow, in heaven and on earth and under the earth, and every tongue acknowledge that Jesus Christ is Lord, to the glory of God the Father (Phil 2:3-11, NIV).

Is it not ironic that Jesus' success came backwards? In contrast to the world, the Kingdom of God operates upside down. It reverses the natural flow of success. To get to the top floor of God's palace, we cannot jump on an elevator and press the button to the penthouse. Nor can we find the stairwell and climb up to the top. Instead, we must take the stairs *down* to the basement.

But once in the basement we discover that, somehow, our downward climb to the lowest floor got us to the top floor. Our descent to the cellar was a supernatural and paradoxical ascent to greatness in God's Kingdom. That's the route Jesus traveled. He emptied Himself, going from low to lower. Then His success came backwards. When He went down, God raised Him up.

Part of Jesus' descent was His deliberate change of form. Paul tells us that Jesus' appearance did not bear the obvious, physical traits of His divinity. During His earthly life, our Lord looked like a typical first-century Jewish man (because in a very real sense, He was a typical first-century Jewish man). He was so familiar that his fellow Nazarene villagers could not get used to the wisdom and power flowing from the neighborhood boy they had known as young Yeshua ben Yosef.

To the Jewish mind, based on Old Testament stories, if God appeared to people, the sight would normally be resplendent, otherworldly, and terrifying, thus qualifying those who saw Him for some great prophetic ministry—or death. To the Greek mind, someone of divine origin or majestic station deserved glory and homage (Acts 14:13; 19:28). But to appear as a mere mortal, *and then to take the station of a peasant or slave*, was scandalous to both minds.

Yet Jesus boldly took the opposite form of what people expected as divine. His humility was defined by His willingness not to look great in the world's eyes, but to be content looking great in God's eyes alone—not like the One who created the cosmos, but like one who served tables and died outside the camp. The public face of humility in God's Kingdom is the form of a servant among people.

But it was not enough that Jesus changed form. He also had to conform His life to His Father's will. He had to obey His Father's wishes. "Although He was a Son, He learned obedience from the things which He suffered" (Heb 5:8). Jesus changed form and then lived a life of obedience. This simple truth is a rebuke to the pride lurking deep in the unregenerate human heart.

I had a friend who, before he surrendered to Jesus, experienced God for the first time when the Spirit spoke directly to his heart, commanding him to do something specific. My friend was shocked, not primarily that the God of the Universe would actually talk to Him, *but that God would dare tell him what to do.* He was the prototypical modern man of his age, the kind of rebel whose free spirit motto was, "No one tells *me* what to do." Yet God's still small voice invaded my friend's soul and introduced the radical idea that he did not belong to himself. He belonged to the One who was now laying claim to His life. From that point on, he was no longer the master of his own destiny; he was the servant of Another.

Yet that was the way Jesus lived his whole life. Though He was God's eternal and beloved Son—heir of time, space, and eternity, King of Israel and Lord of all—He did not live His life on His own terms. He lived like an obedient Son who belonged to His Father. No matter how great He was (actually, because of how great He was) He offered Himself to God in absolute submission.

Further, Jesus served with the *spirit* of a servant. His outward actions of service corresponded to a deep, inner attitude of submission. Jesus did not lower Himself to the depths of servitude begrudgingly. He did not serve against His real wishes. Rather, according to Paul's words above, Jesus had the perspective that He was called to use His greatness, not first for His own good, but for the good of others. The very purpose of Jesus' greatness was to use that greatness to be an effective servant. He joyfully put Himself in the place of a slave to wash people's feet. He was the Lord yet had the attitude that He should serve… because He knew that's what Lords do.

It's a daring and convicting concept: *Jesus treated sinners like they were more important than Him.* Of course that does not mean He was a lesser person than they. Jesus was in fact equal to God, and He knew it. But instead of using that knowledge to dominate sinners, He used it as the occasion to serve them. He treated the needy like they were nobles at a great banquet and He was the household steward appointed to serve them.

> Jesus, *knowing* that the Father had given all things into his hands, and that he had come from God and was going back to God, rose from supper. He laid aside his outer garments, and taking a towel, tied it around his waist. Then he poured water into a basin and began to wash the disciples' feet (John 13:3-5, ESV, emphasis added).

Jesus did not insist on the honor He deserved. Rather, His sense of honor gave Him confidence to treat others like they were VIPs and He was their servant. Jesus did not have the mindset that others should serve Him; He had the mindset that He should serve them. Which is the same attitude that enabled Him to die for sinners.

Follow the Leader

According to Phil 2:3-11, Jesus is the Hero of humility—the *true* Hero for believers to admire and imitate. Therefore, that same passage serves as a template for us. It offers some powerful, practical tools to help us imitate Jesus' heroic humility:

<u>View relational friction as God's golden moment to serve others</u>. This takes faith. Usually when we have a conflict with someone, it's hard to humble ourselves and look for ways to serve the person who hurt us. "He wronged me and should be humbling himself to *me*, not the other way around." But relational strife, no matter who's at fault, is the very occasion that calls for humility in God's Kingdom.

Ordinary humility is convenient. Heroic humility is sacrificial.

Paul described Jesus as the Hero of humility in the specific context of relational conflict (compare Phil 2:1-2 with 4:2-3). His urgency was to reunite people in the local church whose relationships were fractured by self-centered attitudes. So Paul's description of Jesus' humility acted like cement between damaged bricks in God's house.

One of the most important occasions to enter humble service is when someone hurts you (keeping in mind that such humble service may include confronting the other person in a spirit of gentleness; see Matt 18:15; Gal 6:1). If you find yourself in the midst of discord, see it as a moment designed by God to serve heroically. Even though God did not cause the conflict, His providence now defines it as the opportune time to wash the feet of those who wronged you *and thus repair the relationship.*

Don't insist on your rights. Remember Jesus. He emptied Himself of outward dignity and looked the part of a lowly servant. Likewise, we are called to bless those who wronged us at the risk of making them look right. Radical humility does not serve its own reputation; it serves the needs of others at its own expense. Then it trusts God with its public image, just as Jesus did.

Heroic humility goes beyond forgiveness. It views offense as God's call to serve.

<u>Make true happiness your goal</u>. Contrary to our natural inclinations, ultimate happiness does not come when we serve our own interests first. True happiness comes when we serve the interests of others. Radical humility brings real joy. Let's look beyond the inconvenience and see the joyful reward of serving others. Jesus washed His disciples' feet and told them He was their example. Then He said: "If you know these things, *you are blessed if you do them*" (John 13:17, emphasis added).

One of the great treasures of God's Kingdom is the family of relationships we enter when we are born again. He designed us in such a way that we need healthy family relationships with the body of Christ to grow spiritually. There's no way around it. When those relationships are intact, we experience a kind of satisfaction that does not come any other way. That's why Paul told the Philippians that their unity through humility would complete his joy (Phil 2:2).

On the other hand, strife burdens our hearts with anger, sorrow, or guilt—unnecessary weights to carry in life. Too many of God's people choose to live without restoring broken relationships because they're not willing to humble themselves and make things right.

But reconciliation and robust friendships in Christ restore God's joy to our hearts. And that joy is worth the sacrifice of humbling ourselves and serving those with whom we have conflict. When we cherish our family in Christ more than we cherish our own rights and reputations, we experience God's delight in a special way.

In addition to creating powerful relationships, humility brings joy because it yields tremendous rewards in God's Kingdom. Though we cannot earn salvation, Scripture teaches that believers are rewarded in the age to come for the life of humility they live now (Matt 5:3-10).

Jesus received from God the highest name specifically because He humbled Himself during His earthly life (Phil 2:9). We, too, are promised greatness in God's Kingdom if we humble ourselves (Matt 20:26-27; 23:12). When eternity is real to our hearts, it brings us great joy to anticipate the rewards of the age to come. Such anticipation gives us God's joy now, and that joy enables us to humble ourselves and serve.

When we make this kind of happiness our goal, it's easy to follow our Leader into radical humility.

<u>Obey the Lord's command</u>. One of our most effective tools for cultivating radical humility is to remember that it is the Lord's requirement. When faced with the temptation to let our own desires divert us from humbly serving others, it is helpful to recall this simple rule: selfishness is not allowed in God's Kingdom. Jesus said, "If you love Me, you will keep My commandments" (John 14:15).

The Bible tells us candidly to "do nothing from selfish ambition or conceit, but in humility count others more significant than yourselves" (Phil 2:3, ESV). In other words, just do it. Sometimes the inspiration isn't there to serve with radical humility. That's when we refocus on Jesus' example and adore Him through our sheer obedience.

<u>View other people as your superiors</u>. This may sound strange at first, but it captures the heart of radical humility. Selfishness instinctively thinks of itself as superior to others. The flesh says, "Me first." But the Spirit and the Word advise the opposite: "Value others above yourselves" (Phil 2:3, NIV).

We must make a radical reversal in our minds just as Jesus did. He knew He existed as equal to God. But He took on the mindset of a servant, treating sinners throughout the world as if they were more important than He! We need the same attitude. To love people is to treat them with the utmost value.

However, the Bible's command to treat others as more important than ourselves is not a command to look down on ourselves. It is rather a command to look up to others.

Jesus did not look down on Himself. He existed in the form of God, after all, and knew His unlimited value. Indeed, Jesus' knowledge of His eternal value is the very thing that enabled Him to wash the feet of His disciples (John 13:3-4). Jesus knew who He was, where He came from, and where He was going—to the highest place over all creation. Paul's emphasis, then, is not on our *in*feriority; it is on others' *su*periority. We must see others as the dignitaries we are called to serve.

Listen to King David's attitude toward the subjects in his kingdom: "I say of the holy people who are in the land, 'They are the noble ones in whom is all my delight'" (Psa 16:3, CSB). Can you imagine a king in our world with that perspective? Is history not filled with violent conflicts and horrible injustice because rulers scorned their subjects, using them for their selfish purposes rather than honoring and serving them? Yet David saw his subjects as honored dignitaries he was appointed to serve. He looked up to them. In God's Kingdom, the very mindset of royalty is the mindset of a servant who serves his subjects.

Notice that Paul does not tell us to regard others as superior only if they deserve it. (Did we deserve Jesus' radical humility and heroic service when we were sinners?) No, Paul directs the command *to us* to fulfill our calling to service. He does not direct it to others to deserve our service. People are not worthy of our service based on their behavior. They are worthy of our service based on the radical love and humility in our own hearts. A royal heart is a humble heart. And a humble heart sees others as nobility, worthy for us to serve.

Act saved. A lifestyle of humble service is the chief fruit of our salvation. Notice what Paul says right after his description of the Hero of humility:

> Therefore, my beloved, as you have always obeyed, so now… work out your own salvation with fear and trembling, for it is God who works in you, both to will and to work for his good pleasure (Phil 2:12-13, ESV).

God works salvation in us when we believe. There is nothing we do to earn this indescribable gift. But He then calls us to work out this salvation through imitating Christ's radical humility in the power of the Spirit.

What greater demonstration of our salvation could there be than our imitation of Jesus' selfless service? That is the mark of the King's cross, so it becomes the mark of the King's people. The very thing we were saved to do was to live like Jesus. Therefore, if we really have received the gift of His salvation, let us act that way. Let's work out the salvation that He worked in: the very character of the humble King.

Become Like a Child

When Jesus needed to instruct His disciples about humility, He surprised everyone by calling on one of the least as an example:

> At that time the disciples came to Jesus and asked, "Who, then, is the greatest in the kingdom of heaven?" He called a little child to him, and placed the child among them. And he said: "Truly I tell you, unless you change and become

like little children, you will never enter the kingdom of heaven. Therefore, whoever takes the lowly position of this child is the greatest in the kingdom of heaven. And whoever welcomes one such child in my name welcomes me" (Matt 18:1-5, NIV).

During the time of Jesus, social status was very important. People desired public honor and despised public shame. They wanted to be celebrated as much as their positions would allow—for their connections to important people, donations to community service, or positions in the government or a special organization.

It's no surprise, then, that the disciples would be concerned about who is the greatest in the Kingdom. God's reign was breaking into the world through their Master, Jesus. They expected Him to enter Jerusalem and reveal Himself as Messiah. Surely He would muster an army, overtake the Empire, establish His throne, and appoint His new government. Then the disciples would be His highest-ranking officials—those who would compose the royal court and rule the world with Him.

So naturally, they wanted to know who might have the highest positions on that royal court. "How," they were asking, "do you get to be among the greatest in Your Kingdom?" The way Luke tells it, the disciples were actually arguing about who should have the highest rank on Jesus' royal court (Luke 9:46-48). Perhaps they were debating questions like: Who had the longest history with Jesus? Who performed the greatest miracles? Who spent the most time alone with Him? Who was given the most responsibilities? Whose loyalty and skill would place him above the rest?

But here's something important to keep in mind: though the disciples were acting arrogantly, they were also behaving normally within their cultural context. Questions of "Who's the greatest?" were quite expected in a culture that was so conscious of status. So, yes, their question smacked of pride, but it also reflected the values of their social habitat. The disciples thought they had an unusual opportunity to climb some rungs on the ladder to success, so they contended for the top position.

For that very reason Jesus put a child in front of them and called them to be different. He wanted to rebuke their pride and reform their natural thinking about greatness. A child had no social status. A person's youth meant subordination. Children were totally dependent and required to serve the wishes of their household's father. Surely Jesus could not be telling his adult disciples to take such a position on purpose! They had already grown out of that naturally lower rank, and now they were about to rule the world.

But it was true. Jesus was basically saying, "My Kingdom is different than other kingdoms; it does not define greatness as the world does. You must change your ambitions. Become the ones of lowest rank who serve others, without any thought that it should be otherwise. Leave the rest to God who will reward you in the age to come." This must have shocked the disciples. Jesus was calling them to a personal revolution. He was not merely calling them to be humble; He was breaking the basic rules of life in their world. He was turning everything upside down. He was telling the disciples that they must give up the kind of honor their world held dear in order to experience His kind of honor. They had to lose everything to follow Him into true greatness.

Marks of the Cross

Children had no official position in a household or government (Gal 4:1-2), no political leg to stand on, no leverage over others, no social rank. But that was the position Jesus taught His followers to take. They had to learn that the values of God's Kingdom were antithetical to the values of their world. Their new culture measured success differently than their old culture. They had to change their minds, alter their outlook, embrace a whole new code—the code of a culture where the last were first and the first were last.

To experience the power of Jesus' cross, we too must learn this lesson. Just as Jesus shocked His disciples by comparing their roles to children, so must He shock us. We need our natural aspirations for power and prestige, whatever form they take, to be transformed into aspirations for lowliness and servitude.

Our modern culture has its own version of status-consciousness. It exalts the wealthy, beautiful, and talented as the most valuable. Those with physical resources and charismatic personalities are given the greatest worth, attention, and power over others—sometimes even in the church. However,

> God has chosen the foolish things of the world to shame the wise, and God has chosen the weak things of the world to shame the things which are strong, and the base things of the world and the despised God has chosen, the things that are not, so that He may nullify the things that are, so that no man may boast before God (1 Cor 1:27-29).

In God's Kingdom, children rule.

Our natural minds need renewal. The core values of our hearts must be deeply converted to those of God's Kingdom. Under divine government, children are exalted, servants are honored, and the meek inherit the earth. The rule of Jesus Christ advances through an entirely different set of rules than the kingdoms of this world. Let's renew our minds. Let's change and *become like little children.*

The Greatest in the Kingdom

The human heart naturally longs for greatness. The disciples were not proud simply because they wanted to be great. Their pride was in the *way* they wanted to be great: by exalting themselves at the expense of others. Jesus corrected that notion by putting a child before them and essentially saying, "Become great *My* way."

The disciples' desire to be great was not wrong in itself. Only their *reason* for desiring greatness (to be honored over others), and their *mode* for attaining greatness (self-serving competition) were wrong. But the craving for significance, in and of itself, was not bad. Jesus actually invited them to be great. "Whoever takes the lowly position of this child *is the greatest* in the kingdom of heaven" (Matt 18:4, NIV, emphasis added). Jesus did not shun greatness; He embraced it. What He rejected was the desire to be great on the world's terms and through the world's means.

If this sounds odd, look closely at another example. In an episode similar to this one, James and John vied through their mother for the highest positions in Jesus' Kingdom. "Command that in Your Kingdom these two sons of mine may sit one on Your right and one on Your left" (Matt

20:21). When the other disciples heard about it, they were furious. Jesus stepped in to correct the root of their misguided aspirations for greatness, as well as their argument. But notice how He made His correction. He did not say, "Whoever wishes to be great is self-centered and needs to repent." Rather He said, "Whoever wishes to become great among you shall be your servant, and whoever wishes to be first among you shall be your slave; just as the Son of Man did not come to be served, but to serve, and to give His life a ransom for many" (Matt 20:26-28).

Jesus did not invalidate His disciples' natural wish to be great. He identified and harnessed it. But He did correct the sinful pride that would seek greatness through the world's means and for the world's reasons. The spirit of the world seeks to inspire us to exalt ourselves at other people's expense (Luke 22:25; Gal 4:17-18). Yet the reason God makes His people great is to serve others. Our desire to be great should become our desire to take the lowest position to serve people sacrificially. That is the purpose for greatness in God's Kingdom. That is the message of our King's crucifixion. God exalted Him because He lowered Himself. He rose because He died.

With this in mind, consider these verses that reveal how God originally designed His people for greatness and then redeemed us for greatness:

> Then God said, "Let Us make man in Our image, according to Our likeness; and let them rule..." (Gen 1:26).

> [God said to Abraham,] "I will make you a great nation, and I will bless you, and make your name great; and so you shall be a blessing" (Gen 12:2).
>
> What is man that you take thought of him, and the son of man that You care for him? Yet you have made him a little lower than God, and You crown him with glory and majesty! You make him to rule over the works of your hands (Psa 8:4-6).
>
> As for the saints who are in the earth, they are the majestic ones in whom is all my delight (Psa 16:3).
>
> For You formed my inward parts; You wove me in my mother's womb. I will give thanks to You, for I am fearfully and wonderfully made. Wonderful are your works, and my soul knows it very well (Psa 139:13-14).
>
> Jesus told his disciples, "Whoever keeps and teaches my commandments, he shall be called great in the kingdom of heaven" (Matt 5:19).

God-given greatness gives us courage to serve others. We don't need the praise of people to define us. We don't need to overcome other people to feel powerful. Authority comes from God. He designed us for significance and redeemed us for greatness. When we realize this, we can afford to live the life of service to which He called us. Look again at Jesus' example:

> Jesus, *knowing* that the Father had given all things into his hands, and that he had come from God and was going back to God, rose from supper. He laid aside his outer garments, and taking a towel, tied it around his waist.

Then he poured water into a basin and began to wash the disciples' feet and to wipe them with the towel that was wrapped around him (John 13:3-5, ESV, emphasis added).

See the connection? Jesus was able to serve His disciples from the lowest position, not in spite of His significance, but because of it. May God give us grace to do the same.

As Innocent as Doves

We have seen how God esteems the inherent, humble social position of children. The code of His Kingdom runs counter to the code of the world. God exalts the humble and humbles the exalted. But there is another, related characteristic—a virtue, really—that draws God's attention, affection, and friendship like few other things. It is the natural purity of a child.

Heaven loves innocence.

Yes, all humans are born with sin. "Foolishness is bound up in the heart of a child" (Prov 22:15). Children are inherently sinful and selfish as fallen humans, and even their early behavior reflects this in many ways. Yet, paradoxically, children have a natural naiveté about evil. Compared to the big, corrupt world around them, they are relatively simple, honest, and trusting. They have not yet learned the grander dynamics of dishonesty or the bad manners of manipulation. Though they will have to deal with the selfishness emerging from within, and though the world will increasingly seek to pour them into its mold, they have not yet experienced a commitment to corruption that corresponds to their environment. They are children, relatively untainted by evil. They are innocent.

God *loves* this innocence. He loves *children* because of this innocence. And He has a special place in His heart for those people who, somehow, though they have grown up in this stubborn, rebellious world, have preserved a measure of their childhood innocence.

> Jesus saw Nathanael coming to Him, and said of him, "Behold, an Israelite indeed, in whom there is no deceit!"
>
> Nathanael said to Him, "How do you know me?"
>
> Jesus answered and said to him, "Before Philip called you, when you were under the fig tree, I saw you."
>
> Nathanael answered Him, "Rabbi, you are the Son of God; you are the King of Israel."
>
> Jesus answered and said to him, "Because I said to you that I saw you under the fig tree, do you believe? You will see greater things than these" (John 1:47-50).

What a powerful scene this is. Jesus recognizes in the Spirit the same innocence in Nathanael that characterizes His own, guileless soul. The two immediately connect. Their hearts join in a genuine conversation of the noblest kind. There is no hint of self-consciousness, no trace of ulterior agendas. In a short, tight dialog, their meeting reaches a depth of friendship and mutual clarity virtually unknown in this self-obsessed and suspicious world.

Their interaction becomes God's abode, that community of innocent ones that the prophets predicted (Mal 3:16) and among which God has always longed to dwell (Isa 4:3-6; Ezek 37:27). "Behold, I and the children whom the Lord has given me are for signs and wonders in Israel" (Isa 8:18). These two men find fellowship in their mutual, childlike innocence, communing together in the chaste, rarified air of loving candor—all to the Father's delight (Luke 10:21-22). By virtue of their shared guilelessness, the two men knew each other in the twinkling of an eye. Jesus instantly saw authentic Israel (see Psa 73:1); Nathanael instantly saw the *King* of authentic Israel. Together they manifested God's Kingdom, a microcosm of heaven on earth.

That is the power of innocence.

And that is what is so lovely to God about children. Only childlike innocence can perceive this kind of royalty. Only children can see God's Kingdom (John 3:3). "Blessed are the pure in heart, *for they shall see God*" (Matt 5:8, emphasis added). Nathanael, a true Israelite, possessed a childlike innocence that opened his inner eyes. Though Jesus had not yet revealed much of His glory, Nathanael *saw* Him, not merely as a prophet or teacher, but as God's own Son, Israel's true King.

Children see the Kingdom. Innocence welcomes the divine.

Innocence, then, is purity of heart—that delightful naiveté of evil that children enjoy. It does not deny that evil exists, nor judge it with an uncaring, religious superiority. Rather, innocence is ignorance of the *experience* of evil, and it continually declines the temptations to learn of it.

Innocence refuses to grow up in the carnal sense, becoming accomplished in the dark, deceitful ways of the "real world."

In other words, innocence knows what evil is, but does not think what evil thinks or do what evil does. This is why, to the core of His being, God is utterly innocent. "This is the message we have heard from Him and announce to you, that God is light, and in Him there is no darkness at all" (1 John 1:5). Jesus is the exact representation of God's nature in human form, the paragon of innocence. He knows what evil is, better than anyone, but does not know what it's like to practice it. He is our example of childlike innocence.

Listen to Paul's words, reflecting the theology of innocence he wishes for his churches:

> In evil be infants, but in your thinking be mature (1 Cor 14:20).

> I want you to be wise in what is good and innocent in what is evil (Rom 16:19).

> Prove yourselves to be blameless and innocent, children of God above reproach in the midst of a crooked and perverse generation, among whom you appear as lights in the world (Phil 2:15).

Now, more than ever, it is time for the church to return to her innocence. To return to innocence is to return to our apostolic witness in the world. "Behold, I send you out as sheep in the midst of wolves; so be shrewd as serpents and innocent as doves" (Matt 10:16).

Let us perceive Jesus' Kingdom afresh and so "change and become like little children." Too often Christians in our generation test the boundaries of godly virtue. They think true freedom is to be like the world as much as possible—in the name of spiritual liberty—without stepping over the edge into blatant sin (all while the "edge" is usually a movable boundary line according to convenience).

Christians who engage in this spiritual brinkmanship may avoid big sins like physical murder and adultery, but freely use foul language, engage in slanderous gossip, or carouse with little restraint. They glory in their freedom as an abstract concept, rather than as a Person with an innocent heart, very clear values and, yes, household rules. (Would their version of "freedom" work in a marriage?) Then they look down on others who do not share their knowledge of extravagant grace. To them, these old-fashioned Christians are actually legalists who do not understand the real gospel and whose spiritual experience consists merely of rules, regulations, and fear.

But even if (and I emphasize, if) the "liberated" Christians are technically correct about some of their liberties, isn't their entire *disposition* lacking the one virtue in which God so delights? Are they not trying to live near the edge and sustain a complex moral argument at the expense of their innocence? The whole spirit of their debate is to see what they can get away with, rather than to learn what pleases the Lord (Eph 5:10). Doesn't this pattern, then, reveal the deeper issue of a subtle corruption in the guise of spiritual freedom?

Innocence, on the other hand, is a precious, powerful virtue in God's Kingdom. Its attitude leads us to convictions and behavior that reflect a way utterly free of legalism, yet still happily obedient to the Word, blameless, and holy in God's sight. *Childlike innocence is pure delight*—delight in God's own moral translucence. It is a sensitivity to God's countenance, sensing His blush at the slightest hint of evil, and then blushing with Him (see Jer 6:15; 8:12).

This is why innocence attracts God. It creates an ambience of divine camaraderie and joy unsullied by the world's little corruptions. "You have *loved* righteousness and *hated* lawlessness; therefore God, your God, has anointed You with the *oil of gladness* above Your companions" (Heb 1:9, emphasis added). According to the New Testament, that is true freedom (1 Cor 8-10; 2 Cor 11:2-3). That is the innocence embodied by Jesus. Those who follow Him, who change and become like children, are those upon whose shoulders that sensitive, dove-like Holy Spirit alights with comfort and confidence (Matt 3:16).

May we be those children.

Jesus Said: Change

Humility is not an automatic virtue. Jesus realizes that those who come to Him are not already the way they should be. They do not yet bear the traits that characterize Him. So He tells His disciples they must *change* and become like children.

This is both an invitation and a challenge.

It's an invitation because Jesus recognizes our need for transformation. We do not have to make ourselves innocent in order to come to Him. We receive His innocence as a gift and then grow into it by the sanctifying presence of the Holy Spirit. That is what discipleship is. The fact that Jesus even appeals for us to change means we are off the hook of performance. It tells us that He does not reject us for failing to be like children before we come to Him. He realizes what we are and *invites* us to change and become like children. Such an invitation to change implies, "Come as you are."

But it also implies, well, change. That is the challenge. It says, "Come as you are, but do not remain as you are." By God's grace, become what you are not. Become like a child. Restore innocence to your soul. Yes, Jesus requires us to become radically different. But how is this possible? How is it possible for people all grown up and shaped by this sinful world system to return to a deep, childlike innocence? It is only possible by the grace of God and the power of the Holy Spirit.

We cannot change without God's power, yet Jesus still directly commands us to change. That means the innocence He gives us as a gift requires our willing submission to and cooperation with the process of becoming innocent. Listen to these words again:

> Therefore, my beloved, as you have always obeyed, so now, not only as in my presence but much more in my absence, work out your own salvation with fear and trembling. For it is God who works in you, both to will and to work for his good pleasure. Do all things without grumbling or disputing, that you may be blameless and innocent, children of God without blemish in the midst of a crooked and twisted generation, among whom you shine as lights in the world (Phil 2:12-15, ESV).

Let's look again at this point that bears repeating. Paul well captures the tension of grace as divine, transforming power.

God is the one working in us, yet *we* must work with Him to translate our free gift into daily life. We work out what God worked in. *We* obey. *We* must do all things without grumbling and disputing. Yet it is *God* who grants us His presence to do so.

It is like a rich father who gives his daughter a beautiful new sports car as a gift. It comes with a powerful engine and gift cards for free, unlimited gasoline and service. The daughter did not buy it nor build it. She does not even have to know how the fuel, spark plugs, and pistons work together to make the engine perform. And she certainly does not have to make them operate herself. That is all given by her father's grace.

But she must drive the car.

If she does not, that great gift goes nowhere. Or if she only drives it down her driveway, or in the close vicinity of her neighborhood street, she will never experience the potential of her father's powerful, free gift. That part is up to her. She must steward the grace given her and *work out* her new car's vast capabilities in the world and inside the rules of the road.

So must we cultivate the innocence that God has placed inside us. God has given us an entirely new life with the powerful engine of His new nature—the nature of a child untainted by evil. But we must learn to drive it. That takes time, prayer, relationships, mistakes, recoveries, trials, and long-term commitment. Change and *become* like children.

Once we realize that the engine of innocence is within us, we may carefully and consistently exchange old thoughts and habits for those of a child of God. When we recognize a pattern of behavior that is contrary to the sweet meekness of Jesus, we can repent and build a new pattern. It takes practice, as well as the encouragement and correction of our spiritual family. But with time and focused dedication in the Spirit, the change comes and increases.

So let's be deliberate and watch over our hearts for behavior tinged by guile. Perhaps we are prone to gossip, or we subtly slander others to feel better about ourselves. Maybe we complain quietly or simmer with jealousy when others receive blessings we wish we had. Or perhaps we harbor hidden, unclean behaviors. These are not the ways of innocence. These are not the ways of Kingdom children.

That is when Jesus calls us to Himself and says, "Change and become like children." Take hold of your new, God-given identity as an innocent child. Repent of carnal, "grown-up" behavior and thoughts. Allow the Holy Spirit to work in you a new ignorance of the ways of evil. Value the innocence that God loves. Arise as His innocent children to be examples of purity in an impure world.

After all, the Kingdom of Heaven belongs to such as these.

5

FORGIVENESS

Forgiveness is one of the defining marks of the cross. It left scars on Jesus' body that tell the story of His love, the price He paid for our pardon. Indeed, His scars sketch the outline to one of the most beautiful aspects of His character. When we then take up our cross, that same mercy must mark us too. Forgiveness is a sacrifice that leaves a scar on our soul. It marks the loss of our old person's carnal justice in exchange for the new creation's mercy.

Jesus' death was an act of radical forgiveness that revealed God's heart. While His enemies were crucifying Him, Jesus prayed for them, "Father, forgive them; for they do not know what they are doing" (Luke 23:34). This is a staggering thought: Jesus suffered *our* punishment to forgive us for sins we committed *against Him*.

> Very rarely will anyone die for a righteous person, though for a good person someone might possibly dare to die. But

God demonstrates his own love for us in this: *While we were still sinners*, Christ died for us (Rom 5:7-8, NIV, emphasis added).

The cross is a statement about God, by God. It reflects His unselfish, loving heart. He is, by nature, a forgiving God. Even from the endless ages of eternity past, the cross was burning at the center of His passions. He is "a God merciful and gracious, slow to anger, and abounding in steadfast love and faithfulness, keeping steadfast love for thousands, forgiving iniquity and transgression and sin" (Exod 34:6-7, ESV).

Not only does the cross express God's nature, but it also provides the means for our forgiveness in the blood of Jesus Christ:

> Indeed, under the law almost everything is purified with blood, and *without the shedding of blood there is no forgiveness of sins* (Heb 9:22, ESV, emphasis added).
>
> This is my blood of the covenant, which is poured out for many *for the forgiveness of sins* (Matt 26:28, ESV, emphasis added).
>
> In him we have redemption through his blood, *the forgiveness of sins*, in accordance with the riches of God's grace (Eph 1:7, NIV, emphasis added).

No sin is too great, no crime so wicked, that it extends beyond the reach of Christ's blood to forgive. People may refuse the blood of this great Savior. They may trample it under foot, or harden their hearts against its power (Heb

6:6; 10:29; 1 John 5:16). In so doing, they reject the only substance precious enough to redeem their eternal souls (1 Pet 1:18-19). But those who come to God in penitent faith experience a washing so deep in the soul—a cleansing of guilt and conscience so absolutely thorough—that words fail to describe the joy of its effects.

> For if the blood of goats and bulls and the ashes of a heifer sprinkling those who have been defiled sanctify for the cleansing of the flesh, how much more will the blood of Christ, who through the eternal Spirit offered Himself without blemish to God, cleanse your conscience from dead works to serve the living God? (Heb 9:13-14).

All followers of Jesus have experienced the transforming power of His forgiveness.

Before we met Christ, we had no moral compass. "Among whom we all once lived in the passions of our flesh, carrying out the desires of the body and the mind, and were by nature children of wrath, like the rest of mankind" (Eph 2:3, ESV). We took advantage of people for our own gain. We blasphemed. We indulged lusts. We lied and cursed without restraint. But the moment we believed Him, in that fraction of an instant, He erased a lifetime of massive guilt. Our debt was paid, our heart cleansed, and our life born again.

That is the power of Jesus Christ's blood! He has covered the sins of even the vilest sinners who have bowed their knees to Him in repentance and faith. Rebellion, adultery, murder, stealing, self-righteousness, slander, lying, and perversion—all forgiven, wiped clean, thrown into the blood-red sea of divine remission. As the old hymn says, "His blood can make the foulest clean, His blood availed for me!"[1]

Behold the power of Christ's cross. It expresses God's revolutionary love—His willingness to forgive the most heinous sins against Him—but it also provides the eternal means to do so. We must always remember His cross of forgiveness. "All have sinned and fall short of the glory of God, and are justified by his grace as a gift, through the redemption that is in Christ Jesus, whom God put forward as a propitiation by his blood, to be received by faith" (Rom 3:23-25, ESV).

Because of God's immeasurable gift of forgiveness, we now carry the responsibility to forgive others. The sheer fact that we are forgiven actually places a call on our lives to be people who forgive quickly and totally. And this is more important than we may realize. It is surprising how many who claim to follow Jesus continue to harbor bitterness or resentment against those who have hurt them. Too often those who have been forgiven much, forgive little. This ought not to be.

Unforgiveness within the church has caused much damage: ugly conflicts, nasty gossip, broken relationships, church splits, and many times a very poor testimony to the world. If we don't forgive, we don't embrace Christ's cross. And if we don't embrace Christ's cross, we don't walk in His power.

Forgiveness is crucial to walking in victory and experiencing Jesus' authority over spiritual enemies. Further, when we forgive offenses, we encounter Jesus in a more intimate way. This causes us to grow in the knowledge of Him and allows Him to forge His character into ours. We must, therefore, forgive—quickly, eagerly, thoroughly, and incessantly. Scripture shows us how.

Remember Your Own Forgiveness

The fact that an eternally merciful and kind God forgave us for sins committed against Him should motivate us to forgive those who sin against us. Love begets love.

We must realize that our offenses against God were *real*. Our sinfulness was *real*. The risk of eternal punishment was *real*. So His forgiveness was a very, very real liberation for us. It was an indescribable gift. We were sinners; we were guilty and in unspeakable danger. But when we believed, God freely forgave us through Christ's cross. The more we remember this and take ownership of it, the more likely we are to adopt a lifestyle of forgiveness as a debt of gratitude to God (yes, according to Scripture, we should have a healthy sense of indebted obligation to love and forgive others: see below, as well as Rom 8:12; 13:8).

Jesus told an important parable about forgiveness (Matt 18:21-35). A king forgave one of his slaves an enormous amount of debt. The NIV translation calls it "ten thousand bags of gold." That equals about *60 million days of wages* in the ancient world![2] Jesus intentionally made it an extreme amount to illustrate that the sum debt God forgives a sinner is astronomical.

But then that forgiven slave was not willing to forgive his fellow slave a debt of merely "a hundred silver coins." Here was the king's response when he learned about it:

> "You wicked servant," he said, "I canceled all that debt of yours because you begged me to. Shouldn't you have had mercy on your fellow servant just as I had on you?" In anger

his master handed him over to the jailers to be tortured, until he should pay back all he owed."

This is how my heavenly Father will treat each of you unless you forgive your brother or sister from your heart (Matt 18:32-35, NIV).

The debt others owe us will never be as great as what we owed God. The colossal weight He lifted from our shoulders should inspire us to forgive our debtors.

Let all bitterness and wrath and anger and clamor and slander be put away from you, along with all malice. Be kind to one another, tender-hearted, forgiving each other, *just as God in Christ also has forgiven you*" (Eph 4:31-32, emphasis added).

Remember your forgiveness. It will help you forgive others.

Be Sure That If You Don't Forgive, God Won't Forgive You

Christians seem to forget this sobering truth. Sometimes we take selfish advantage of God's original forgiveness, tacitly assuming we have license to hold resentment against someone without affecting our relationship with God. But that's simply not the case, as the previous parable teaches. Jesus states it plainly in the Sermon on the Mount. First He teaches us what to say when we pray: "Forgive us our debts, *as we also have forgiven our debtors*" (Matt 6:12; emphasis added). Then He explains,

> For if you forgive other people when they sin against you, your heavenly Father will also forgive you. But if you do not forgive others their sins, your Father will not forgive your sins (Matt 6:14-15, NIV).

According to this passage, forgiveness is a tremendous responsibility—one that affects whether or not we will experience God's forgiveness in our relationship with Him. When we don't forgive others, God does not forgive us. When we don't show mercy, we assign ourselves to God's place by deciding who can be forgiven and who can't. Specifically, we decide that *we* deserve forgiveness while some others do not.

But we don't have the right to make that choice. God is the only one who can, and He gives mercy to anyone who calls out to Him. So when we usurp God's position in someone else's life by not forgiving him, we lose *our* position of being forgiven in our relationship with God.

We must avoid such presumption. Let's maintain our position as God's forgiven servants by freely offering that same forgiveness to others.

Protect Your Prayer Life

Anger hinders our prayers, while forgiveness releases them to new heights. Notice that, right after two key teachings on *prayer*, Jesus added the warning that we must *forgive* (Matt 6:9-15; Mark 11:17-26; see also 1 Pet 3:7). Read those passages carefully. They clearly imply that if we don't forgive others, then our prayers will not be effective. Grudges jam the lines of communication with God. Forgiveness opens them back up. A core Kingdom principle is that our human relationships have direct bearing on our relationship with God.

> So if you are offering your gift at the altar and there remember that your brother has something against you, leave your gift there before the altar and go. First be reconciled to your brother, and then come and offer your gift (Matt 5:23-24, ESV).

We must realize that God takes our relationships with others personally. If we've experienced a broken relationship, God first requires us to fix it, as much as it depends on us, before we continue in fellowship with Him. In this passage, the harmony of our vertical relationship depends on harmony in our horizontal relationships.

Certainly it is challenging to maintain a good, healthy relationship with everyone all the time. We cannot control what others do. But we can control—we must control—our side of the relationship both in heart and behavior. Thus Jesus taught His followers they must *relentlessly* forgive offenders: "Be on your guard! If your brother sins, rebuke him; and if he repents, forgive him. And if he sins against you seven times a day, and returns to you seven times, saying, 'I repent,' forgive him" (Luke 17:3-4).

The apostles recognized this would be an enormous challenge. They knew that weak human nature could not sustain such a constant level of mercy. It takes a supernatural character through faith to be an "un-offendable" person who walks in constant forgiveness. So they cried out, "Increase our faith!" (Luke 17:5).

Jesus responded, "If you had faith like a mustard seed, you would say to this mulberry tree, 'Be uprooted and be planted in the sea'; and it would obey you" (Luke 17:6). In other words, it requires the same faith to forgive that it does to pray with power. There is only one spring of faith in our hearts. If we have poisoned it with resentment, our prayers for other things will be polluted too. On the other hand, if we exercise the radical faith necessary for relentless forgiveness, then that same faith will enable us to pray successfully for impossible things.

Our prayer life is both protected and empowered when we walk in forgiveness. So let's keep our relationships clear and our hearts free of bitterness. Let's walk by faith by walking in forgiveness. It will make our prayers soar.

Keep Your Sights on the Larger Picture

A challenging but vital Kingdom truth is that God uses other people's faults to build our character. Our response to injury determines our growth in the Lord. We cannot keep our focus on the pain someone has caused us—the betrayal, accusations, injustice, or dishonesty. We must focus on how the Father can use other people's sins to make us more like Jesus.

However, I am not saying God causes people to abuse us. He does not. But when people do hurt us, and some surely will, God can take those bad things into His hands and turn them into tools to forge the image of His Son in us. Though it's not always easy, we must pray that God would give us eyes to see the harm people have caused us from this perspective.

Sometimes even good people do stupid things. Deep friendships will expose us to potential pain. We can't enter genuine relationships without some measure of risk. Humans are imperfect. Like trying to get to our gate on time through a crowded airport, there are times we will cut into the paths of others or even bump into them, or they will bump into us. But if we try to run from such risk, we will miss the more valuable treasures of love. Or if we react to pain with anger and bitterness, we will miss the most precious opportunities to grow into the beautiful character of God's Son.

Love is worth the risk. But we must embrace the biblical perspective and realize that God will use the faults of others to bring about something good in us—and sometimes even for the people around us. Remember the story of Joseph. His brothers treated him with the utmost contempt. Essentially they murdered him, at least in spirit, by ambushing him, selling him into slavery, and lying to their father about his death. Joseph's own brothers abused him out of jealousy and deleted him from their hearts and family to benefit themselves. How could brothers do that? They are the very ones who should have looked out for him and protected him. That's what family does. How could Joseph ever forgive them? Listen to his perspective when they were reunited years later in the royal household of Egypt.

> His brothers then came and threw themselves down before him. "We are your slaves," they said. But Joseph said to them, "Don't be afraid. Am I in the place of God? You intended to harm me, but God intended it for good to

accomplish what is now being done, the saving of many lives. So then, don't be afraid. I will provide for you and your children." And he reassured them and spoke kindly to them (Gen 50:18-21, NIV).

Joseph obtained the strength to forgive his brothers from his focus on God's overall purposes. But this took radical faith. Joseph dared to believe that God used his brothers' cruelty to develop his character and advance a plan to save the world. And that's exactly what happened. Good came out of Joseph's hardships because he was able to forgive his brothers and entrust himself to the Lord.

The same opportunity awaits us when people hurt us. We can make Joseph's story our story. We determine if our pain will turn to anger or glory, based on our willingness to forgive.

View Bitterness and Resentment as the Sinful Lusts They Are

God calls anger a sin and exhorts us to lay it aside. "Let all bitterness and wrath and anger and clamor and slander be put away from you, along with all malice" (Eph 4:31). Anger is the sinful luxury of the unredeemed heart. But for the redeemed heart, it is neither a right nor a virtue.

Without actually admitting it, sometimes Christians live as if anger were not really a sin. We think that as long as we don't commit the "big" sins, like immorality, stealing, or murder, we are living clean lives and can afford some anger in our hearts. But this is not the case. In fact, Jesus connects anger with murder:

> You have heard that it was said to those of old, "You shall not murder; and whoever murders will be liable to judgment." But I say to you that everyone who is angry with his brother will be liable to judgment; whoever insults his brother will be liable to the council; and whoever says, "You fool!" will be liable to the hell of fire (Matt 5:21-22, LEB).

Harboring anger toward a fellow believer (or anyone) is sin, and it is destructive. The slander that oozes out of bitterness has probably "murdered" more reputations, friendships, and churches than even sexual sins. Is it right for Christians to criticize a fellow believer for committing some of the "bigger" sins, while those same Christians angrily slander one another without restraint? The Bible makes no such distinction. Neither should we.

Notice how Paul lists what we might consider the really bad works of the flesh—"sexual immorality, impurity, debauchery, idolatry, and witchcraft"—right next to those we often allow ourselves without the same level of guilt—"hatred, discord, jealousy, fits of rage, selfish ambition, dissensions, factions, and envy" (Gal 5:19-21, NIV84).

Are we ready to take Paul's words seriously? Do we *really* believe that envy, of all things, should be listed with witchcraft or fornication? Is discord, too common among churches today, in the same list as *idolatry*? Yes, actually, it is. And there is good reason for it. *All* the vices in this list are expressions of the old, self-centered nature. *All* are fruits of a fallen humanity at war with God and itself. It's time to identify bitterness as the harmful, sinful disease that it is… and repent.

Listen to what James says:

> What is the source of quarrels and conflicts among you? Is not the source your pleasures that wage war in your members? You lust and do not have; so you commit murder. You are envious and cannot obtain; so you fight and quarrel (James 4:1-2).

Let's listen closely to what this passage is saying. James, like Jesus, associates anger with murder (see also 1 John 3:15). In this case, anger takes on the form of serious disputes among believers. James says they are essentially acts of spiritual murder. They are the kinds of fights that are intended to *eliminate* the other person in some way—by scorning him, devaluing him, or removing him from other people's hearts or friendship circles.

Is not un-forgiveness a way of eliminating a person from your heart? Is not spoken resentment a way of eliminating a person from someone else's heart? Is not this kind of anger, without being addressed and uprooted, the very spirit of murder?

Further, James identifies the birthplace of such disputes: unfulfilled lust. The reason for the quarreling is that people wanted something, but they did not get it—so they got mad. This reaction is not righteous anger. It's the outgrowth of a life ruled by selfish concerns rather than concern for others. Selfishness, then, must have an assistant to serve its interests. That assistant is lust. Lust is the handmaiden of selfishness. It insists that the desires of selfishness must be fulfilled at once.

When lust doesn't get fulfilled, it turns into anger against those obstructing its fulfillment. This anger can take many forms, but they all issue from a heart unwilling to forgive. The point is this. To nurse such attitudes in the heart—to refuse forgiveness for offenses—is *lust*.

But you may ask, "How can my anger be *lust* when the other person hurt me for no reason, and I was totally innocent? Isn't my anger justified? Or at least a natural reaction?" Those are excellent, fair questions. Scripture answers them simply and practically: "Be angry and do not sin; do not let the sun go down on your anger" (Eph 4:26, ESV).

In other words, the natural, initial response to unjust treatment may be anger. The Bible acknowledges that and does not call the anger sin at this point. But neither does the Bible give us license to let that anger shift into angry attitudes, words, or actions. It accepts that anger may be our natural, first response, but then it instructs us to deal with it before it becomes sin. In fact, it tells us to deal with anger before the end of the day.

Then it gives these commands just a few verses later:

> Let no corrupting talk come out of your mouths, but only such as is good for building up, as fits the occasion, that it may give grace to those who hear. And do not grieve the Holy Spirit of God, by whom you were sealed for the day of redemption. *Let all bitterness and wrath and anger and clamor and slander be put away from you*, along with all malice. Be kind to one another, tenderhearted, forgiving one another, as God in Christ forgave you (Eph 4:29-32, ESV, emphasis added).

The anger Paul says we can have without sinning in v 26 is the same anger he says to put away in v 31. We simply don't have the right to do anything with our initial anger except put it away and replace it with love.

We have control over our hearts. God gives us the grace and responsibility to master our emotions before they master us. Often anger deceives us into thinking that, because we have been wronged, then our anger is justified. Since *I'm* the one offended, then I must be right!

Actually, no. When we allow anger to take root in our hearts, we are not accomplishing justice; we are fulfilling lust. And remember: lust is the handmaiden of selfishness. It serves selfish interests at others' expense. It does not serve God's interests (see Matt 16:23).

Therefore, let's have the courage to admit that un-forgiveness is lust. It is the sinful expression of the self-ruled life that God's Kingdom has overthrown and replaced with love. It has no place in the chambers of the redeemed heart. Bitterness is a fruit of the old flesh that should be crucified. On the other hand, forgiveness is part of the righteousness that Jesus died to give us. So let's accept that un-forgiveness is nothing more than a selfish, destructive lust and repent of it. Let's walk the way of our King.

Embrace Your God-given Call To Be A Forgiver

The moment we surrender to Jesus Christ, God forgives all of our sins. That forgiveness, however, is not solely for the purpose of getting into heaven. It is also our *calling to be forgivers*.

When God remits our sins at the moment of salvation, He actually does more than give us forgiveness. He also gives us the Holy Spirit. God grants us His presence in order to engrave His character into our souls. That means salvation is more than a new start; it is a life-altering blast from heaven that transforms us into new creatures. We thus become supernatural people, powerfully able to conform to the image of God's Son.

The very nature of Jesus Christ now resides in the core of our being. His forgiving nature is now *our* forgiving nature. We must then recognize it, cultivate it, and integrate it into our daily lives.

This is one of the chief teachings of the New Testament. "Therefore, if anyone is in Christ, *he is a new creation.* The old has passed away; behold, the new has come" (2 Cor 5:17, ESV, emphasis added). Our old, unforgiving disposition is dead. "We know that our old person was crucified with Him" (Rom 6:6, my translation). But the new person in Christ, overflowing with mercy, is alive! "If Christ is in you, though the body is dead because of sin, yet the spirit is alive because of righteousness" (Rom 8:10).

We must accept by faith that the gracious, loving, kind, and forgiving nature of Jesus Christ now burns like a fire inside of us. Once we accept this, God calls us to fan that nature into the flames of practical behavior. Said another way, we must put our new, forgiving nature on like a new coat. Listen to these powerful exhortations from Scripture:

> Clothe yourselves with the Lord Jesus Christ, and do not think about how to gratify the desires of the flesh (Rom 13:14, NIV).
>
> If then you have been raised with Christ... *clothe yourselves with the new person*, who is being renewed in knowledge after the image of the One who created him... *Clothe yourselves,* then, as God's chosen ones, holy and beloved, with deep compassion, kindness, humility, meekness, and patience, bearing with one another and forgiving each other, if anyone has a complaint against another; just as the Lord forgave you, in the same way so should you (Col 3:1, 10, 12-13, my translation and emphasis).

Forgiveness becomes an increasingly easier habit for us when we realize it is part of our identity in Christ. The day we were born again we became forgivers. As much as our old nature may kick, scream, and lust to get angry and hold on to resentment when someone wrongs us, we have to remember that we are no longer bitter people by nature. Our initial emotions may demand that we are, but we are not.

Rather, by the Spirit, we are loving, forgiving people like Jesus. We must then insist that we will not act like that old, dead, bitter person who is buried and gone. But we will act like the beloved child of God who is alive and well and full of relentless forgiveness. "In the same way, count yourselves dead to sin but alive to God in Christ Jesus. Therefore do not let sin reign in your mortal body so that you obey its evil desires" (Rom 6:11-12, NIV).

Don't let the enemy steal your identity. Remember your new nature. Remember your calling. You are not a person given to bitterness or resentment. Your emotions and actions are not dictated by the behavior of other people. Your emotions and actions are dictated by the nature of Christ within you. Embrace your God-given calling—be a forgiver.

---

1. Charles Wesley, *O For a Thousand Tongues to Sing* (1739).
2. Craig Keener, *The IVP Bible Background Commentary: New Testament*, second edition (Downers Grove: IVP Academic, 2014) 92.

6

THE MARKS OF MATURITY

Life in Tension: Flesh and Spirit

Authentic Christian life involves paradoxes. God's Kingdom is already here, but it is not yet fully here. Followers of Jesus already possess resurrection life, but do not yet possess resurrection bodies. We live now under God's dominion and experience His Holy Spirit in so many glorious ways. Yet we await the Day when Jesus returns and finally makes all things new, establishing His Kingdom on earth as it is in heaven.

Two ages—the coming, glorious age and the present, evil age—are both here and clashing all around us. That means we live in a spiritual war zone, a conflict we feel even within ourselves. Paul tells us why: "For the flesh desires what is contrary to the Spirit, and the Spirit what is contrary to the flesh. They are in conflict with each other, so that you are not to do whatever you want" (Gal 5:17, NIV). Those are powerful, sobering words. Both flesh and Spirit contrast and collide even within our souls. As they vie for supremacy, it is our job to choose our course and develop Christ-like character within the friction.

But that is not bad news; it is good news. The fact that we are in the battle means we are alive. We are no longer slaves to sin, oppressed by spiritual tyrants, ignorant of the truth, or subject to our own selfishness. Jesus has set us free. Not only do we enjoy God's forgiveness, but we also have the power to live like the humans God intended us to be. The Spirit and the flesh may be in conflict, but the Spirit is the Spirit of the almighty Father and His Son, Jesus Christ, the victorious King. "What then shall we say to these things? If God is for us, who is against us?" (Rom 8:31).

People without life in Christ must always obey their mortal cravings. Here and there they may overcome some bad habits, but they are neither alive nor free. Followers of Jesus, on the other hand, have been raised to newness of life and liberated to fight the good fight. That is why Paul exhorts us "that you walk no longer just as the Gentiles also walk...[but rather] you lay aside the old [person], which is being corrupted in accordance with the lusts of deceit, and that you be renewed in the spirit of your mind, and put on the new [person], which in the likeness of God has been created in righteousness and holiness of the truth" (Eph 4:17, 22-24).[1]

Yes, sometimes it is difficult. And yes, we must always choose the way of the Spirit. But thank God we have the choice! Thank God we have the Spirit! Thank God we are in fact completed human beings with freewill and power! Who can calculate the potential of a redeemed man or woman?

This is why Paul puts it so bluntly, exhorting us right before he explains the Spirit-flesh conflict: "Walk by the Spirit, *and you will not gratify the desires of the flesh*" (Gal 5:16, NIV, emphasis added). Similarly in Romans: "So then, brothers, we are obligated not to the flesh, to live according to the flesh. For if you live according to the flesh, you are going to die, but if by the Spirit you put to death the deeds of the body, you will live" (Rom 8:12-13, LEB).

There you have it. There is indeed a battle. The flesh still has cravings that run counter to the new person. Yielding to the Spirit rather than the flesh will hurt our pride and leave the marks of the cross on our souls. But thank God, *we now have the opportunity to share in Christ's sufferings and develop His eternal image in our earthly lives.* What a high privilege and noble existence.

Developing Christ's image during this age of spiritual warfare is just when it counts. We will not have this opportunity after the resurrection. Now is the time—on the battlefield, against pressure, amid temptation—to conform to the image of God's Son. So let's put both hands to the plow and get this thing done. Through it all, we have God's comforting presence, the companionship of the saints, and unlimited power to give us victory. It's actually a very good deal, and it is the meaning of life itself.

That is why I wrote this little book. I wanted to remind us that internal scars are part of new life in Christ. The losses we feel while developing the image of Jesus are not strange occurrences or alarms that something is wrong. They are in fact signs that something is right. We should not be surprised when our flesh craves something contrary to the

Spirit and then feels the loss of its denial. Jesus told us to take up our cross, and that cross will leave its marks.

But Jesus also said to take up our cross *and follow Him*. While denying ourselves is the first part of the equation, embracing the risen Jesus is the second part. He is with us, leading the way through every valley, every battle, every failure, every success, every restoration, every season, every highlight, every lowlight, and every moment in between. We do not merely take up our crosses; we do not merely suffer losses. We also possess the great Alternative as our motivating ambition and empowering presence.

Jesus is the great Alternative.

He is the One we take up our crosses to follow. His cross is not about abstract suffering. It is about *Him*. It makes room for His glory in our bodily lives. Scars from the cross mark those places where we realized Christ's character was worth more than our desires. So like the merchant of fine pearls, when we find that pearl of great price, *we sell all we have to buy it* (Matt 13:45-46). The joy of its greater value energizes us to sell possessions of lesser value. Again we turn to Paul, a man who found this treasure:

> Whatever things were gain to me, those things I have counted as loss for the sake of Christ. More than that, I count all things to be loss in view of the surpassing value of knowing Christ Jesus my Lord, for whom I have suffered the loss of all things, and count them but rubbish so that I may gain Christ, and may be found in Him, not having a righteousness of my own derived from the Law, but that which is through faith in Christ, the righteousness which

comes from God on the basis of faith, that I may know Him and the power of His resurrection and the fellowship of His sufferings, being conformed to His death; in order that I may attain to the resurrection from the dead (Phil 3:7-11).

There's that paradox again. Paul suffers the loss of *all* things—not merely the trophies of his Jewish background, but everything. Yet he gains Someone of such spectacular value that everything now lost gets exposed as refuse anyway. May God help us to apply Paul's testimony to our own lives. When we feel the loss of something we held dear, we actually feel the loss of something desperately temporary and painted with fool's gold.

If our selfish desires become manure in the light of Christ's face, what exactly did we lose? And if those losses leave marks, dare we think those scars disfigure us? Do they not rather beautify us? Does not every scar that marks a loss become an aperture through which resurrection life beams?

People with scars radiate. They shine with the brightness of the sun. The accumulated marks of the cross make mature disciples incandescent.

Paul's testimony confirms the worth of our paradox. The young Nazarene he wanted to know had to suffer death to be raised from the dead, and Paul entered that same reality. He accepted it. He saw that, in Jesus Christ, the two otherwise opposing forces of death and life were united. The two had become one flesh. And Paul knew that, whatever God had joined together, no man could separate.

This is why Jesus' glorified body always bears the scars of death, both literally and figuratively. Paul embraced Jesus as He is, not as Paul would have Him to be. No aspect of Jesus' composite nature could be circumvented. This former Pharisee, upon seeing the blinding light of the One whose surname was Persecuted, liquidated all other assets, died to the old spiritual marriage covenant, and lunged headlong into the bottomless crystal sea of the Mystery that is Jesus Christ—both in His resurrection power and in fellowship with His suffering.

In perfectly paradoxical fashion, the scars of Paul's losses mingle with the glory of new life in Christ. Together they blend to form in Paul's bodily existence the image of the One he loves with all his heart. The same must be true of us.

So welcome the scars that mark the losses of worthless things. Do not fear the threats of the old crucified nature. Always remember the greater value of Christ's image in you. If trading fool's gold for eternal gold leaves marks, be proud of those marks. And consider the option. In the end, fool's gold will be possessed by those after whom it is named. They will die with no scars… and no gold.

"He is no fool who gives what he cannot keep to gain that which he cannot lose."[2]

The Heart of the Matter

The crux of this issue, as I see it, is spiritual maturity. Mature believers, or new believers on their way to maturity, accept the paradox of God's Kingdom as a part of life. They embrace the fact that the forging of Christ's character into their souls will create scars. But they also know that the value of the new way of life exceeds the value of the old life. The scars are worth it.

Immature Christians, on the other hand, do not value the scars. They try to avoid the kinds of losses required to develop Christ's character. To release an offense requires them to let go of anger rooted in a sense of personal justice and reject the lust for vengeance (or at least for a little resentment). To lose business for the sake of integrity requires them to surrender visible reward for invisible reward. To give a large donation in total secrecy requires them to decline the soul's desire for earthly praise. To cultivate true community requires them to give up their role as church shoppers who merely attend services. For spiritual adolescents, such acts of self-denial hurt and cost too much.

It is more important for them to evade such pain and loss than to become like Jesus. Then when they do go through hardship, they waste it by complaining and blaming others, rather than allowing God's master craftsmanship to do its work. Did you know the letter to the Hebrews was written for this very purpose? Immature believers were feeling the weight of their losses, while the author exhorted them to become mature and realize that scars are not strange things. They are rather part of the race to maturity.

> You have not yet resisted to the point of shedding blood in your striving against sin; and you have forgotten the exhortation which is addressed to you as sons, "My son, do not regard lightly the discipline of the Lord, nor faint when you are reproved by Him; for those whom the Lord loves He disciplines, and He scourges every son whom He

receives." It is for discipline that you endure; God deals with you as with sons; for what son is there whom his father does not discipline? But if you are without discipline, of which all have become partakers, then you are illegitimate children and not sons. Furthermore, we had earthly fathers to discipline us, and we respected them; shall we not much rather be subject to the Father of spirits, and live? For they disciplined us for a short time as seemed best to them, but He disciplines us for our good, so that we may share His holiness. All discipline for the moment seems not to be joyful, but sorrowful; yet to those who have been trained by it, afterwards it yields the peaceful fruit of righteousness (Heb 12:4-11).

None of this suggests, however, that unless we are miserable, we are not growing. Quite the contrary. What could be more fulfilling than walking after the Spirit and growing in Christ? When we delight ourselves in the Lord, does He not give us the desires of our hearts (Psa 37:4)? When we abide in Him and His words abide in us, does He not answer our prayers and make our joy full (John 15:1-11)? Scarred Christians are the happiest kind of Christians! For they have invested themselves completely to know Jesus Christ as He is, and they have found Him to be all the Scriptures declare Him to be. They rejoice with a glorious joy, proudly bearing His image.

By emphasizing scars, losses, and the like, I am not being negative. I am instead drawing attention to an important aspect of Christian maturity that is not always readily embraced, yet it is an essential truth—as the Hebrews passage above makes clear. Even as new creations who live under grace with resurrection life, it is still costly to develop character. Mature people take ownership of this truth. They look past their immediate desires and choose to gaze into glory.

When we humble ourselves during a conflict, sacrificing our right to be right for the sake of unity, it will leave a mark. When we lay down our ministry agendas to serve our spiritual family, it will leave a mark. When we roll the burden of financial hardship on the Lord, dare to trust Him, and enter His rest, it will leave a mark.

But maturity recognizes the sheer worth of those marks. For those marks indicate a life lived in love, and love is the vocation of every Christian, the main virtue of the mature (1 Cor 8-10). Just as love left its marks on Jesus' body forever, so it will leave marks on our souls. And these are marks we will never regret. Despise not such scars. Their accrual equals our character, the very personhood we will take into the age to come.

One day we will see Jesus. We will see the scars on His glorified body and understand perfectly the point of the pain. With a greater joy than we can now understand, we will bow our knees at the sight of His ineffable magnificence—His overwhelming, luminous beauty—and behold physical marks of love from which blood and water once flowed, but that now burn like a thousand suns. Knowing it was all for us, we will lift our voices in gratitude for the privilege of having to bear a few scars for Him.

Therefore, let us not be surprised when choices to walk with the Spirit feel injurious and leave their marks. Let's gather our courage and grow up. It's time to stop being selfish and start acting like *Christians*—people worthy of the calling with which we have been called. Scars will come; we can handle it. God is with us. He is *in* us both to will and to do of His good pleasure. May we embrace His cross and join the countless souls before us who placed the highest value on cultivating Christ's image.

> For I consider that the sufferings of this present time are not worthy to be compared with the glory that is to be revealed to us…And we know that God causes all things to work together for good to those who love God, to those who are called according to His purpose. For those whom He foreknew, He also predestined to become conformed to the image of His Son, so that He would be the firstborn among many brethren; and these whom He predestined, He also called; and these whom He called, He also justified; and these whom He justified, He also glorified… But in all these things we overwhelmingly conquer through Him who loved us. For I am convinced that neither death, nor life, nor angels, nor principalities, nor things present, nor things to come, nor powers, nor height, nor depth, nor any other created thing, will be able to separate us from the love of God, which is in Christ Jesus our Lord (Rom 8:18, 28-30, 37-39).

---

1. Here I used the NASB translation, but substituted "person" for "self" to render the Greek word, *anthrōpos*.
2. Jim Elliot, personal journal entry on October 28, 1949, pictured at the following link from the Wheaton College "Billy Graham Center Archives": https://www2.wheaton.edu/bgc/archives/faq/20.htm.

ALSO BY ROBERT J. GLADSTONE

Revival is not God's ultimate goal for His people… the ***biblical church*** is God's ultimate goal! God is calling the body of Christ to return to its New Testament roots.

In *A Time to Build*, Bob offers clarity on the church's identity in light of modern revivals and God's overall plan for history. During seasons of outpouring we experience divine visitation, yet God's purpose is to move from visitation to habitation.

It is time for a Jesus Movement.

It is time to build the house of the Lord.

Order at https://www.thekingspeople.org/build/

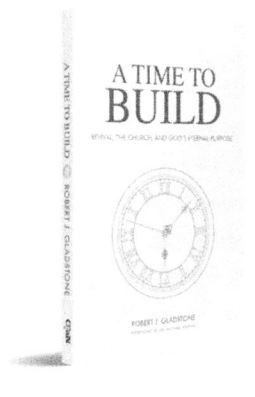

Made in the USA
Coppell, TX
04 April 2024